CREATIVE
CARDBOARD

CREATIVE CARDBOARD

*Making Fabulous Furniture,
Amazing Accessories,
and Other Spectacular Stuff*

LINDA RAGSDALE

LARK BOOKS

A Division of Sterling Publishing Co., Inc.
New York

This book is lovingly dedicated to my children, Nikolas, Tyler, and Jessica. You are my muses. You continually teach and inspire me. You have given me a new pair of rose-colored glasses for viewing the world and the ability to look with my heart. I no longer listen, but I hear. And to my husband, Ben. Without your love and companionship, this world would have less color and less brilliance. I thank God for making us a family. I love you all.

Mom

Editor: **Paige Gilchrist**

Art Director: **Dana Irwin**

Cover Design: **Barbara Zaretsky**

Assistant Editors: **Veronika Alice Gunter, Heather Smith**

Assistant Art Director: **Hannes Matthias Charen**

Editorial Assistants: **Anne Wolff Hollyfield, Rain Newcomb**

Production Assistants: **Amanda Robbins, Shannon Yokeley**

Photographers: **Evan Bracken, Light Reflections, Sandra Stambaugh** (chapter openers)

Illustrator (color illustrations): **Dana Irwin**

Illustrator (technical illustrations): **Bernadette Wolf**

Library of Congress Cataloging-in-Publication Data

Ragsdale, Linda
    Creative cardboard : making fabulous furniture, amazing accessories & other spectacular stuff / by Linda Ragsdale
        p.   cm.
    Includes index.
    ISBN 1-57990-219-7 (pbk.)
    1. Paper work. 2. Paperboard. I. Title

    TT870 .R23 2002
    745.54—dc21   2001038516

10 9 8 7 6 5 4 3 2 1

Published by Lark Books, a division of
Sterling Publishing Co., Inc.
387 Park Avenue South, New York, N.Y. 10016

© 2002, Linda Ragsdale

Distributed in Canada by Sterling Publishing,
c/o Canadian Manda Group, One Atlantic Ave., Suite 105
Toronto, Ontario, Canada M6K 3E7

Distributed in the U.K. by Guild of Master Craftsman
Publications Ltd., Castle Place, 166 High Street, Lewes, East
Sussex, England
BN7 1XU
Tel: (+ 44) 1273 477374, Fax: (+ 44) 1273 478606, Email:
pubs@thegmcgroup.com, Web: www.gmcpublications.com

Distributed in Australia by Capricorn Link (Australia) Pty Ltd.,
P.O. Box 704, Windsor, NSW 2756 Australia

The written instructions, photographs, designs, patterns, and projects in this volume are intended for the personal use of the reader and may be reproduced for that purpose only. Any other use, especially commercial use, is forbidden under law without written permission of the copyright holder.

Every effort has been made to ensure that all the information in this book is accurate. However, due to differing conditions, tools, and individual skills, the publisher cannot be responsible for any injuries, losses, and other damages that may result from the use of the information in this book.

If you have questions or comments about this book, please contact:
Lark Books
50 College St.
Asheville, NC 28801
(828) 253-0467

Printed in Hong Kong

ISBN 1-57990-219-7 (pbk.)

CONTENTS

The Cardboard Diving Board

When you think of cardboard, your imagination may not race into high gear. As a matter of fact, the opposite probably happens. You're likely to think of cardboard as something you might ship fine art in, not something actual art could be made of. Cardboard has long been thought of as nothing more than a packing and storage material. It's shoved under beds, stuffed with sweaters, or stacked in garages, bursting with old files.

No longer. It's time to break out of the box and look at cardboard in a whole new way. In the pages that follow, we'll peel away the layers and look at the rolling paper flutes that make cardboard not only structurally strong but also artistically inspiring. We'll fold, trim, and curl cardboard into fun, fashionable, and fabulous shapes. In other words, we'll dive in.

When I told my son Nik how I see this book—as a creative diving board for cardboard—he tossed off the typical teenage response: "Cool." But, as my words percolated through his very preoccupied mind, his delayed response was: "What? I don't get it." Since this is my first year speaking "teen," I used slow, broken phrases in answering him, "Dive in... immerse yourself..." Aah...the light bulb flicked on. The idea is to become absorbed in the creative possibilities of something you might typically cast aside—all very similar to what I try to encourage with Nik and his homework.

Consider this book a pool of ideas beckoning you to dive in. Its logical progression through four project chapters builds your technical skills and continually encourages you to develop your own style. The Diving Board columns that accompany each project tempt your spirit of adventure. They offer glimpses of the endless ways to embellish your cardboard creations, whether you're into stamping, beading, decoupage, or collage.

The first project chapter, The Boardwalk, introduces you to projects that feature basic cardboard cutting, folding, and assembly techniques. We'll use these techniques to make everything from vases and bowls to wallets and jewelry. The second chapter, A Leg Up, focuses on some clever shortcuts and interesting embellishing ideas for projects such as hanging lights, gift boxes, display columns, and wall sconces. In the third chapter, The Plunge, we'll crush, tear, and otherwise manipulate board into pieces that masterfully disguise their cardboard roots—imagine blooming roses and mums, a woven mirror frame, even a mobile phone case. Finally, in The Big Splash, I present a collection of designs for some show-stopping home decor pieces—from a classic room divider to a dramatic fainting couch.

My intent with every project is to show off the natural beauty and flexibility of cardboard, including all the colors and textural choices available today. I also want to demonstrate what an ideal material cardboard is for all sorts of creative play. It's inexpensive, so dabbling with it won't drain your art budget (and you can spend what you save on extravagant embellishments). It's easy to manipulate, whether you're approaching a project that's simple or elaborate. And it has a very receptive surface—you can paint it, print on it, even woodburn it.

I know what you're thinking. How did a nice girl like me end up in cardboard, when I should be in diamonds or silk? My love affair with the cardboard box started when I was designing cardboard displays for the video industry. As I learned more about the creative possibilities of cardboard, I began inspiring others to see beyond its usual forms and functions, and I haven't stopped since. Once you see it anew, cardboard—that familiar and easy-to-find material—will become a medium that draws you in until you're listening to your own creative impulses.

So, the pool is open. This book is my personal invitation to you to dive in.

BOARD BASICS

CARDBOARD HAS A COUPLE OF NAMES AND A LOT OF DIFFERENT LOOKS. LET'S START OFF BY CLARIFYING THAT *CARDBOARD* AND *CORRUGATE* ARE THE SAME THING. THE PAPERBOARD INDUSTRY CALLS IT CORRUGATED, THE GENERAL PUBLIC CALLS IT CARDBOARD. NO DIFFERENCE. TOMATO, *TOMAAHTO*.

The internal structure of cardboard is the fluting. These soft ripples of paper are held together between two outer sheets of paper. Fluting is measured in letters, with A flute being the largest, and B, C, E, and F identifying the other flutes in descending order of height. The strongest cardboard standing vertically is A flute; it's also least common. B flute is the strongest for horizontal stacking. B and C flute are the most common, because they're used to make standard cardboard boxes. The outer sheets surrounding the fluting come in varying paper weights, including the same weight as that used for the fluting. They can help strengthen any flute.

Cardboard is manufactured in single, double, and triple layers, in all qualities and flute sizes. In addition, there's a current craft craving for decorative single-face cardboard. Here, flutes are exposed and attached to a single back sheet. Single face is especially easy to roll if you're rolling in the direction of the flutes. We'll explore that technique in several designs. Wave board has ripples that cross the board in a wavy pattern. You can also find waffle board and a board that has a bric-a-brac pattern. Crimped paper has no backing, but features an impressed ripple pattern. (You can also emboss cardboard with your own patterns with a variety of tools and techniques I'll tell you about later in this chapter.)

And the colors! Of course, you can find cardboard in its natural, light-brown shade (called kraft cardboard). But it also comes in pastels, brights, and new shades to match home decor trends. You can find cardboard with color-printed sheets laminated onto it, as well. This type is typically used in packaging for toys, small appliances, and similar items, and ordinarily comes in B and E flute. If you've got access to some, work it into your designs. Projects will take on another character with this material. Imagine the Curlicue Curio Cabinet (page 104) made from boxes used to package toys, or the United We Stand Divider (page 91) made with kitchen appliance boxes.

How far out of the box are we going? Far!

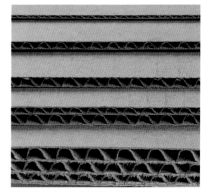

THE INTERNAL STRUCTURE OF CARDBOARD IS FLUTING. THE FLUTES SHOWN TOP TO BOTTOM HERE ARE: E FLUTE, B FLUTE, AND C FLUTE, DOUBLE-WALL CARDBOARD MADE OF B FLUTE AND C FLUTE, AND TRIPLE-WALL CARDBOARD MADE OF TWO LAYERS OF A FLUTE AND ONE LAYER OF C FLUTE.

SINGLE-FACE CARDBOARD, TOP TO BOTTOM: E FLUTE, B FLUTE, AND C FLUTE

METALLIC B-FLUTE SINGLE-FACE CARDBOARD

SINGLE-FACE CARDBOARD IN KRAFT (IN VARYING
FLUTE SIZES) AND VARIOUS DECORATIVE COLORS

SINGLE FACE, WAVE BOARD, AND
WAFFLE BOARD (ON TOP)

WAVE BOARD IN A VARIETY OF COLORS

CARDBOARD WITH COLOR-PRINTED SHEETS OF PAPER
LAMINATED DIRECTLY ONTO THE BOARD OR PRINTED DIRECTLY ONTO BOARD.

GETTING BOARD

So how do you get cardboard? You can find the smaller pieces you'll need for many of the book's projects at your local craft or art store.

Craft stores sell packages of 8½ x 11-inch (21.6 x 27.9 cm) sheets of decorative-flute cardboard and 8 x 10-inch (20.3 x 25.4 cm) sheets of E-flute single-face cardboard in various colors. You'll usually find these packages in the scrapbooking section. You can also find single sheets of decorative-flute board in specialized scrapbooking stores, where there's typically a wider color selection.

Art stores carry large single sheets (typically 28 x 36 inches [71.1 x 91.4 cm]) of E flute single face and of wave board. You can find the sheets in kraft and in an array of colors, including gold and silver. Some art stores are also now carrying 36 and 48-inch tall (91.4 and 121.9 cm) pieces of kraft B and C flute single face, which is more traditionally sold by industrial packaging and moving centers. The advantage is that art stores will sell it by the foot.

Check parent-teacher stores and party stores, too. They sometimes carry large rolls of decorative, single-flute cardboard in printed patterns, the kind used for classroom decorating and bulletin board backgrounds. They also carry rolls of trim. For cardboard with printed patterns, shop office supply stores for file boxes and discount stores that sell cardboard storage containers.

For some of the projects, you'll need larger pieces of cardboard. The best way to find them is to engage in the thrill of the hunt. You can get cardboard from large department stores that have appliance boxes from their floor samples. The cardboard bins at "club stores" are another good source. And recycling centers can be cardboard gold mines. Get to know the folks who run them, and have them hold aside some board for you. They may even be able to tell you where their larger boards come from, and those people can become sources for you. As a last resort, you can purchase mirror boxes and large boxes from mailing centers or moving-and-storage companies.

As much as possible, I've designed the book's projects so they can be made with easily attainable pieces of cardboard.

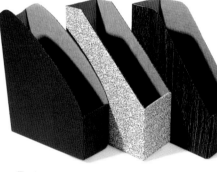

FILE BOXES AND STORAGE BOXES ARE A GOOD SOURCE OF PRINTED CARDBOARD.

STANDARD CARDBOARD BOXES CAN SUPPLY YOU WITH THE RAW MATERIAL YOU NEED FOR MANY PROJECTS.

CARDBOARD TOYS: TOOLS AND SUPPLIES

In the cardboard playground, the basic tools and supplies make work seem like fun. I'll list those that I use, but you know the saying about different strokes. You may already have your favorite tools and supplies for cutting, folding, and gluing. Use those you're comfortable with, if you know they'll accomplish the same task. Otherwise, consider the following toys to make your play more fun.

THE BOARD NECESSITIES

These are the tools I consider essential to my cardboard-crafting sanity (or, some may argue, insanity).

Metal T-square. Its sole purpose is to keep you, your pencil, and your craft knife moving in straight and perpendicular lines.

Large and small plastic triangles. They guide your pencil lines and are key in finding centers and marking angles. Make sure your triangles are large enough to mark the size of your project dimensions all at once; realigning a line is difficult (no need to court difficulty when it's easy to avoid). I use two right triangles, one 12 inches (30.5 cm) tall and the other 18 inches (45.7 cm) tall. You can find triangles with different angle measurements and adjustable angles. A word of caution: These triangles are not for cutting. Once you cut into your triangles, they can no longer be trusted. The best you can do then is hang them as ornaments.

Rulers. I adore metal rulers to cut and measure with; they can handle anything. If you're using another type of ruler, invest in a good metal straightedge as well. I'm not as wild about measuring tape (which also happens to be my thighs' worst enemy). You will need it, though, for checking perimeters on certain projects.

Self-healing cutting mat. This is a wonderful invention. It saves your tables and floors. If you're making only one or two projects, you can use a large, thick piece of chipboard or even cardboard instead of purchasing a cutting mat, but when you're cutting into a material that retains the cuts, you have to be extra careful. The blade of your craft knife may catch in one of the undercuts, which could misdirect the line you're cutting. Check your cutting mat often and flop it over to the clean side regularly.

Bone folder. Paper artists use bone folders for scoring. We'll do the same, and we'll use this handy tool for crushing cardboard as well.

Erasers. Erase those lines away (a face can only hope!). I use soft lead when marking on a board and a pink pearl eraser to remove the marks. You'll need to test any eraser you plan to use, because all boards will hold lead differently and some erasers may leave a residue. There's no remedy for eraser residue. Try saying that three times fast, but don't try an unchecked eraser on your board!

Craft knife. Never start a project with a dull blade in your craft knife. I always keep an extra box of blades nearby for quick changes and the heavy-duty jobs. When cutting triple-wall cardboard, you'll go through a lot of blades. They should always be sharp (have I said this enough?). It's very hard to recut a pulled edge caused by a dull blade. (I admit it, I've learned this through experience.) Your blade should have a handle you can cut straight with. Any type of handle that interferes with your straight-edge or ruler could cause "Project Fling" (see the box below).

PROJECT FLING is the phenomenon that occurs on the rare occasion when a slip of the knife, a torn edge from a dull blade, or some other quirky mistake ruins hours (or sometimes just minutes) of work. Suddenly, your flubbed project, with the mysterious assistance of your own hand, takes wing and rockets helplessly toward the nearest wall. No project has yet to survive this flight.

SHARP PENCIL. And I do mean sharp, needle sharp. I use soft lead, because it's easier to erase. I'm constantly sharpening, because a thick line can make the difference between accurate and close when you're marking out a project. Can you use a mechanical pencil? I don't, but that doesn't mean it won't work for you. Just don't use a lead that is so hard it will cut into your cardboard.

SCRAPER. This is a must for spreading a thin layer of glue over any area. You can make one from a piece of shrink plastic or scraps of cardboard, or even use the sort of plastic display piece earrings are sold on. It should be approximately 3 inches (7.6 cm) square, and its main characteristic should be a straight edge you can use to scrape evenly.

SCISSORS. Scissors are a blade option when you're working with smaller fluted board, such as E flute, and the decorative boards. I used nice sharp scissors in large and small sizes on many of the projects in the book.

CIRCLE AND OVAL MAT CUTTER. When cutting curves, a mat cutter is the answer. It's a somewhat expensive tool (about the equivalent of a nice dinner out for two) but well worth the cost if you're cutting a large quantity of circles or ovals. Its beveled edge provides an added benefit when you're cutting graduated layered shapes, such as the circles for the Vase

USING A CIRCLE MAT CUTTER

Rubenesque, page 28. You can achieve a variety of looks by matching or alternating directions of the beveled edges.

PAPER CIRCLE CUTTER. A paper circle cutter cuts only circles and is meant for cutting paper stock, but you can transfer its skills to cardboard in two ways. A paper circle cutter will cut circles out of

decorative-flute cardboard, which is thin. If you're working with thicker board, you can use the paper circle cutter to make a blade groove to start a circle cut, then finish the cut with your craft knife.

POWER CUTTING TOOLS. Plugged in? If you're working on larger projects, such as the Ms. Divine Divan fainting couch, page 113, you'll want to be. Power tools, such as circular saws and jigsaws, offer the best blades for cutting triple-wall and prelayered cardboard. There are power tools specially made for crafters of all skill levels, so don't be afraid to find one; there's no happy way to hand-cut large, thick pieces. Follow the manufacturer's guidelines on all power tools. Make sure you've set up a worktable that supports your cutting and

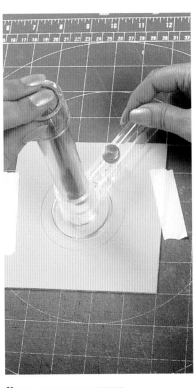
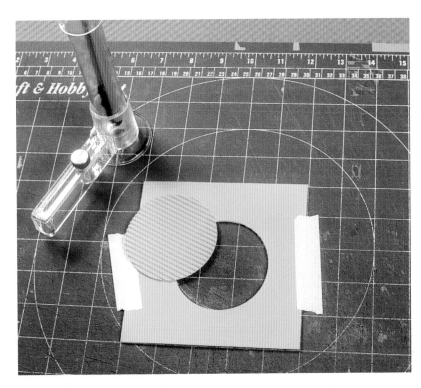

USING A PAPER CIRCLE CUTTER

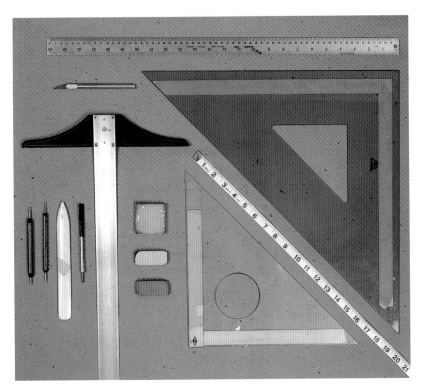

the mobility of the tool. Also, try all sorts of blades or bits when cutting cardboard with power tools. There isn't a bit specific to cardboard, so depending on your tool, its speed, and other variables, one bit may be more effective than another in giving you the edge you're looking for. Some produce soft, "furry" edges, others give you crisp, clean cuts.

BASIC TOOLS, CLOCKWISE FROM TOP: METAL RULER, LARGE PLASTIC TRIANGLE, TAPE MEASURE, SMALL PLASTIC TRIANGLE, ERASERS, METAL T-SQUARE, CRAFT KNIFE (ABOVE T-SQUARE), STYLUSES (FOR EMBOSSING), AND BONE FOLDER

GLUES, SEALERS, AND SCRAPER TOOLS

STICKING TO IT: GLUES AND SEALERS

Viva la Preference!

When it comes to glue, go with your preference. I use two different types of glue. One is a craft glue and the other is a craft cement. I use thick craft glue for layering pieces of cardboard and attaching appliqués on top of them. I use cement when I'm working with metallic cardboard (see the Tin Punch Party lanterns, page 62) and when I'm mixing cardboard and nonpaper materials, such as metal jewelry findings, plastic beads, and other nonporous objects. I also apply my craft glue primarily with my fingers (cement dries too quickly for this), while you may prefer

glue guns or brushes and sponges. I say choose whatever, but pay attention to whether the glue adds any depth to the final assembly so you can figure it into your measurements.

Sealed with a...?

A sealer provides a protective coat to your projects, and each type has distinctive properties. Some sealers prevent water damage, others retard yellowing. Some have a flexible finish, others dry hard and will crack if they're coating moving parts. A sealer's qualities are usually amply shouted on the label in perfect sales pitchese. Know what you want from your project and its function and wear, and the decision will be easy. The rule of thumb—as with

most choices throughout the book—is to go with your preference. I use brush-on sealer; my sister likes spray. She likes matte finish; I like high gloss. Test a few types, then choose what you like best. Seal any project you want to have some extra durability.

GREAT IMPRESSIONS

Here are descriptions of optional tools you can use to make a personal mark on your cardboard's surface.

EMBOSSERS. Putting our best surface forward is easier today with the variety of different embossing tools available. At any craft store, you can buy paper embossers that make everything from flutes and circles to hearts and crosshatch patterns. These handheld tools are easy to manipulate. Their only limitation is the width of the piece they can impress. A pasta machine offers the ability to specifically place impressions (you'll find I have a lot of use for kitchen utensils...outside the kitchen!).

STYLUSES. Another handheld tool for making impressions is a wood or metal stylus, the type used for paper embossing. The large, round, smooth heads of styluses are perfect for detailing. Wooden styluses are also great for cleaning glue that overruns the borders of projects. If you've got short nails, cleaning glue this way also saves your skin from "adhesive cling," where you touch the

PAPER EMBOSSERS AND EVEN PASTA MACHINES CAN BE USED TO MAKE ALL KINDS OF IMPRESSIONS ON CARDBOARD.

EXAMPLES OF SOME OF THE DECORATIVE-EDGE SCISSORS AND SPECIALTY HOLE PUNCHES NOW ON THE MARKET

glue, the glue sticks to you, and you stick to the project or, even worse, you leave a glue fingerprint on the project surface.

DECORATIVE-EDGE SCISSORS AND HOLE PUNCHES. These paper-crafting standbys allow you to create intricate patterns with simple cuts. You can find scissors that cut borders ranging from zig-zags to Victorian curlicues and hole punches in an array of sizes and every shape imaginable. Use scissors and punches together on a piece, and the design options are endless.

FOOLIN' WITH THE TOOLIN': TECHNIQUES

(WARNING: skipping this section may harm your walls! Refer back to "Project Fling," page 11.)

With tools in hand we're ready to...to put them down and keep reading. I know you're eager to get started, but the information in this section will help you decide exactly how and where to start on each project. That said, though techniques are important, they should be viewed basically as guidelines. Review the ones I've outlined here. Try them. If they don't work as well as another approach you know of, by all means adapt them.

BEING MINIMINDED

Before you start any project, take the time to build a miniature version (or "mini") first. The process will help you see how everything goes together. Simply photocopy the pattern, without increasing it to the size you need for the actual project, and fit the pieces together with transparent tape. Building a mini also helps you identify "blind zones." These are areas that are hidden under folds or covered up by other pieces in the assembled project. If, when working on your full-size project, you experience a slip of the knife or notice an unsightly squashed something on your cardboard, look at your mini. You'll be able to determine if the area involved is covered up in a later step—meaning you don't have to worry about the mistake.

Minis are also an aid when you're altering the size or piecing of a pattern. You can note where all the depths of board change and adapt lines or folds if necessary. Forgetting added depths is the main reason for "Project Fling." There's nothing worse than spending a lot of time carefully cutting each line, carefully folding, and carefully scoring, then finding that your folds don't go together.

BLOWING IT OUT OF PROPORTION

It's easy to create the minis and the book's smaller projects, but what about when you move onto full-size projects like the couch, or the chair? How do you increase those itty-bitty patterns from the back of the book to the size you need? Technology offers some easy solutions. The most common is your local copy center: Check to see if they can enlarge your patterns for you. Some have large-bed copiers and even blue-print machines that can handle the job. An advanced copier can "tile" a pattern or print it out on standard 8 1/2 x 11-inch (21.6 x 27.9 cm) sheets of paper that you then piece together. You can also tile a pattern using a computer art or document program with a tiling option in the print mode. To do so, download the patterns first from www.larkbooks.com. Other

places you might be able to have patterns enlarged include blue-print outlets and printing companies.

At the same time that you're taking advantage of all technology offers, don't trust it completely. Hand-check the measurements and layout of your enlarged patterns to make sure they match those specified in the project instructions. Don't simply assume that the dimensions of your pattern have maintained their integrity for the entire enlarging journey. Some copy machines distort, some copy machine operators push wrong buttons, some percentages don't scale correctly—whatever the cause of incorrectly sized patterns, the solution is to catch mistakes before you start using the patterns to cut cardboard.

Note that when you enlarge patterns a great deal, the lines of the patterns become much thicker. When you use them to cut pieces out, cut on, in, or next to the lines consistently on all the pieces.

TRANSFERS TO SUCCESS

How do you transfer a 6-foot copy—or, for that matter, a 6-inch one—from paper to cardboard? First, no matter what size your pattern, cut away any extraneous paper. If we don't need it, we don't need to see it. Next, if you have one main pattern piece you'll use to cut multiple cardboard pieces, make multiple copies of the pattern piece.

Next, you've got three options for transferring your patterns to cardboard. Whichever you choose, be sure to transfer all the pattern markings to the cardboard, too, with a light pencil or pins to mark key points. They tell you where to score, where to fold, etc., when you're later assembling your pieces. (For scoring, another option is to leave the pattern in place temporarily and score right over it.)

■ Option #1: Write On

This is the inexpensive alternative to carbon-paper transferring; you use your pattern copy rather than carbon. Rub the side of the tip of a soft lead pencil along the pattern lines on the back of the copy. Make sure you create a thick line. Tape the pattern in place on the cardboard, rubbing side down. Use a pen or pencil to trace over the pattern lines. This leaves a light, erasable lead line on the cardboard to cut from. If you opt for carbon paper, make sure you can erase the lines. Position the carbon paper under the lines you want to trace. Make sure that the copy and the carbon paper are secure, so they won't move while you're transferring.

■ Option #2: The Applied Rule

A second method of transferring is to cut out your pattern, apply it to the cardboard with a removable glue, and cut around it. Rubber cement is a great removable adhesive for this purpose. When you're finished, you can remove it with a rubber cement eraser, or you can roll it off with your clean fingers and bounce the little balls around for amusement. Not many glues have this play value! The way I learned to apply rubber cement was to coat the two gluing surfaces with a thin layer of the cement, let it dry, then press the pieces together. Cut out the cardboard piece, using the pattern as a guide, remove the pattern, and clean up the residue. Be sure that you glue the pattern to the correct side of the cardboard. And you don't have to coat the entire piece with rubber cement (what a relief when you're working on something as large as the fainting couch!). Just use enough cement to keep the pattern in place while you're cutting.

■ Option #3: The Cloning Principle

For transferring multiple decorative appliqués, you can use The Applied Rule (above), or you can fashion some templates. Thick card stock or shrink plastic that has not been cooked are good template materials. Shrink plastic makes durable templates that can weather spills, tears, and pets. Another nudge here: Take the time to make sure your templates are accurate. Mark the right side of the template, and note which way you need to lay it down, following the pattern or instructions.

■ Be^2

When you're scoring, folding, and cutting cardboard, it's definitely hip to be square. Sometimes the slightest inaccuracy can prevent the project from assembling correctly. Or, after all your work, maybe your project assembles, but it has that distinctive Leaning Tower of Pisa look. Not a look to strive for.

When you're cutting or scoring cardboard, first line up the flutes of your cardboard on a surface that's perfectly square, such as a lined cutting mat, and tape it in place (photo 1). Your cardboard flutes can be either aligned with or perpendicular to the square line. Then, use a T-square or a triangle to square your pattern on your cardboard, following the flute direction on your pattern, if one is specified. Line up a line on

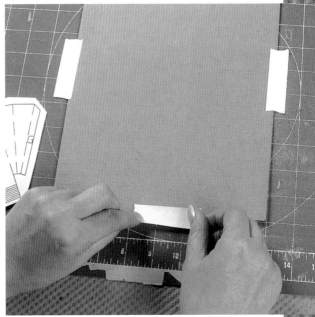

Photo 1

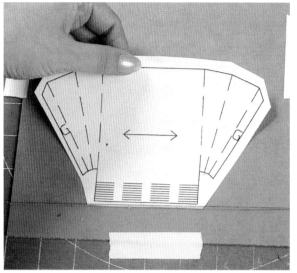

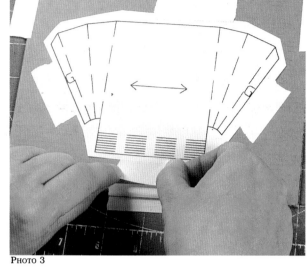

PHOTO 2

PHOTO 3

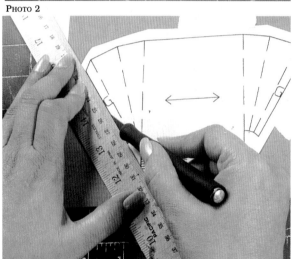

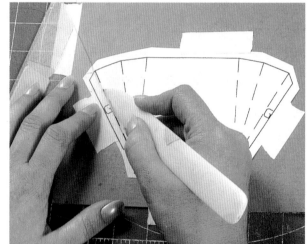

PHOTO 4

PHOTO 5

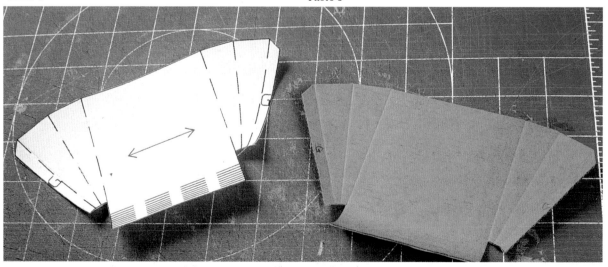

PHOTO 6

18

the pattern with a line on the cutting mat (photo 2). Transfer, tape, or rubber cement the pattern in place (photo 3). Finally, make all your cuts and scores, following the markings on the pattern (photos 4 through 6). If you plan to be doing a lot of cutting and want an even more stable setup than a lined cutting mat, purchase a small, portable drafting table with squared sides.

Several projects in the book call for cutting your cardboard on a 45° angle to the piece's flutes. To do so, align your board as you would for any project, with the flutes running parallel or perpendicular to your square line. Using your right triangle or a compass, lightly mark a line at a 45° angle from the board's squared edge. Cut along the line, then realign the board so the new cut line becomes the edge you square up.

CUTTING

Cutting cardboard is a skill that improves with practice. Some people cut better horizontally. Others like to cut vertically. Learn what works best for you, and lay your patterns out accordingly. And, as if you haven't heard it before, you'll be able to make much cleaner and accurate cuts with a sharp blade in your craft knife. As you cut, use a metal ruler or T-square as a cutting guide; both keep your blade moving straight, but you can't cut into them.

To start a cut, line up your blade with the line you're cutting, making sure the blade is directly on the line. Run the blade over the line to make a cutting groove, then continue to cut until you've severed all the board's layers.

There are two ways to cut a curve; neither approach has to do with racing. The first is to run your very sharp blade over the curve, making a cutting groove, then slowly go back over the curve with your blade until you cut it out. The other is to make your groove, let the curve hang off the edge of your cutting table, and run the blade in and out of the line, sawing the curve. This method also works for cutting out odd and inconsistent shapes. When you cut curves, remember to hold your blade straight unless you want a beveled edge. A beveled edge will change your piece's dimensions, because one edge will sit farther out than the other.

SCORING

Scoring is most commonly used to get a piece of cardboard to change directions. It can also be used as a decorative accent. You typically want to make score lines on the back side of your piece, except in cases when you need lines on both sides of the board, such as when you're scoring an accordion fold.

Not all cardboard scores the same way. Some boards, particularly most decorative boards, need special attention. Wave flute is wonderful, but requires a little more manipulation. You can score it on either side, but when folding, you should crush the waves along the score, so there is minimal tearing. Thicker cardboard needs to be scored more firmly. Single-face board offers a simple ridged texture and can be scored easily on

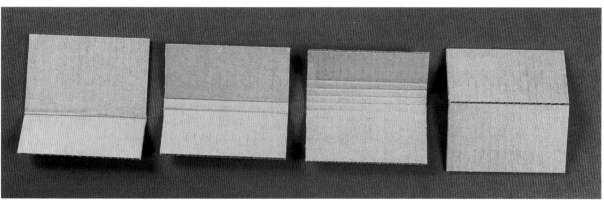

STANDARD SCORES, LEFT TO RIGHT: SINGLE STRAIGHT SCORE, DOUBLE STRAIGHT SCORE, MULTIPLE STRAIGHT SCORE, SLIT SCORE

either side. When scoring a line parallel to the flutes, you will have to crush a flute if your line runs on top of it.

Accurate scoring is vital to project assembly. Scores fold better when you score across your cardboard's flutes. That's not possible on all projects, however, specifically those that require you to fold a piece of cardboard into a box shape. In those cases, it's especially important to pre-fold your score lines; score well, then finish your scores by folding them.

We'll use the following types of scoring throughout the book.

Single Straight Score

This is the most common type of score. A T-square or metal ruler, a bone folder, and a premarked scoring line are all you need to make an accurate single straight score. Align the straightedge along the premarked line, taking into consideration the width of your bone folder, to make sure you'll be scoring right on the line and not beside it. Gently run the bone folder down the line while holding the straightedge in place. Run the tool along the edge several more times, applying more pressure each time, then set the fold by bending the board up from behind, keeping the straightedge in place to ensure the board follows your score. Finally, remove the straightedge and fold the board completely over, pressing down on the fold line.

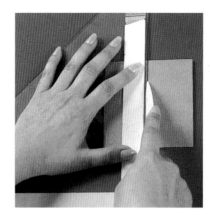

SCORING AND FOLDING A STRAIGHT SCORE

Double Straight Score

This scoring method creates a spine or finished edge, necessary when you're making boxes. It's simply a pair of single straight scores made close together; usually the space between the two should match the thickness of your cardboard. You can also use a double straight score to accommodate another thickness of cardboard, such as a flap, in a fold by increasing the amount of space between the two lines of the score. After scoring your two lines, fold them over one at a time, and run your bone folder over the back of each, establish-

ing a crisp fold line. When you assemble the piece, run your bone folder over the assembled edge again.

Multiple Straight Score

Multiple scores allow you to round a corner in a softer, more gradual way than you can with a single or double straight score. The process is the same as the one for creating the other straight scores; you just make more of them. Then, rather than folding the board to set the scores, roll it back and forth to shape the roll for your project. Single-face cardboard curves around corners naturally, without scoring, if you're curving in the direction of the flutes, because there's no top sheet of paper to hinder the rolling. Cardboard featuring multiple scores won't lie completely flat when you glue it onto another surface; the thickness of the board and the spacing of the scores determine how smooth the roll will be. Be sure to take this into consideration when you plan

DOUBLE STRAIGHT SCORE (LEFT) AND MULTIPLE STRAIGHT SCORE

20

your measurements for a project.

Slit Scores

A slit score is just what it sounds like, a score made by a slit. It allows a board to be folded over so it lies flat against itself. Slit scores take a little practice; try some on scrap board before you cut right into a project piece. Mark your score line, then use a T-square or metal ruler and a very sharp craft knife to slice gently through the surface of the board and the layers of fluting, without cutting into the board's final layer of paper. Crack the

A SINGLE SCORE (LEFT) BENDS, WHILE A SLIT SCORE CAN LIE FLAT AGAINST ITSELF.

board back, and fold it back on itself. Because the fold reveals the interior of the board, you end up with a more attractive spine if you cut across the flutes.

If you cut too deeply when making a slit score, you can rescue your piece—as long as it doesn't have to hinge in the final construction—by cutting all the way through it and gluing one portion directly on top of the other. If

your piece needs to hinge (maybe it's the door to a cabinet, for example), create a tape hinge to rejoin the two portions of the piece. Cover both with a layer of craft glue and kraft paper or a piece of a grocery bag, using the paper to re-create the layer of paper you mistakenly cut through. If your project has another door that needs to match the first one, cut and cover the second door in the same way, to keep the sides even.

Curved Scores

We use standard scoring techniques to create two types of curves in this book's projects: eased curves and dimensional curves.

A straightedge is of no use when you're making curved scores. Either use a template, or make your scores freehand. If you use a template, gently trace your bone folder along the edge of the template several times, each time adding a bit more pressure. Without a template, mark your scoring line. Start by gently running your scoring tool along the line, making a slight indentation, and continue, increasing the pressure as you go.

Eased Curves

You create an eased curve in cardboard using the same technique you use to ease fabric around a curve when you're sewing. After scoring your curved line, cut a border around your piece ½ inch (1.3 cm) outside the

score. Crush the border area with the side of your bone folder to make it more malleable, then, with scissors or a craft knife, slice into the border area in even increments, creating thin tabs, which you glue down when easing your cardboard curve into place.

Dimensional Curves

We use dimensional curves to make the eyes on the Mask of Gazelle-Da project, page 86, making scores on both sides of a single piece of cardboard. Again, you can score using templates or pattern pieces or working freehand. After making the scores, you'll need to gradually pull the scores out of the appropriate side of the board by pinching them up until the board retains the shape you're trying to achieve.

Some Thoughts on Scoring

While we all seek perfection, we won't find it when it comes to scoring. Cardboard, which is made of recycled materials and a variety of glues, can feature all kinds of manufacturing imperfections. That means no matter how skillfully you score, your cardboard may tear. This is a fact, not a theory, so relax. At the point of a tear, you have several options: 1. Throw the board across the room and do a primitive yell and dance. 2. Turn the board over and score on the back side of the score to alleviate board stress. This will not remove the tear, but it stops you from tearing any further. You can then turn the board back over and continue. 3. Use the tear as part of the design (the distressed look, how trendy). 4. Collage or decoupage over the tear. 5. Use your mini (the model you made of your project; see page 16) to remind yourself (if you're lucky) that the torn piece won't be visible in the end.

SEAMS LIKE A WINNER

Seaming sounds like a sewing term, but you won't have to touch a needle to seam two pieces of cardboard together. You'll use this technique when you can't find a piece of cardboard long enough to meet your project's requirements. Some decorative boards, especially, come only in small sizes.

Seaming Single Face
Single face can be seamed almost invisibly if you work in the direction of the flutes. On the end of one of the two sheets you're seaming together, cut up the center of a flute near the edge (photo 7). Separate the backing from the flutes, and pull it off in a thin strip (photo 8). Apply glue to the backless flutes, and gently lay the edge of the other piece on top of them, aligning the backing seams (photo 9). Use your bone folder or your fingers to burnish and smooth the top flutes, express excess glue, and seal the seam (photo 10). You'll seam single face to come up with pieces long enough to wrap around bases for the Make a Stand columns, page 51, and the Hangin' Around lanterns, page 58.

PHOTO 7

PHOTO 8

PHOTO 9

PHOTO 10

When you're wrapping a piece of single face around something, you'll also use a seaming technique to close the circle of your wrap. Run a line of glue along the edge of the piece to which you're applying the wrap, and begin pressing the wrap in place. When you come to the end of the wrap, make sure you have two or three flutes that will overlap onto the beginning of the wrap. Peel off the backing from these two or three overlapping flutes. Run glue on the back of the overlap flutes, and burnish them over the first flutes at the beginning of the wrap to close it.

Seaming Cardboard
Peel away about three flutes of the top sheet of paper from one of your boards. Start at a corner and slowly lift the sheet. Cut and peel so that the seam line falls at the peak of the flute. Clean away any stray paper out of the flutes. Repeat the process with your other board, so the two pieces nest. Run glue into both sets of open flutes, and press them together until the glue sets. If you're seaming two boards that have color on one side, you'll need to peel away the top layer on one piece of board and the bottom on the other. This will also be necessary if the boards you're seaming have exterior papers with different thicknesses.

The connection won't be invisible when you seam together cardboard that isn't single face. Also,

22

the seamed pieces won't be as solid as a single piece of board, so don't use this technique in a situation where strength is critical— better to go find a longer piece of cardboard.

STICK AND STACK

Layering cardboard provides pieces with both strength and dimension. We use this technique to strengthen the base of the Ha Ha Ha Hall Light, page 54, and to sculpt the shape of the Whirlwined wine holder, page 43.

Precutting your pieces makes layering most shapes, even the most intricate, a simple endeavor with accurate results. First, stack your cut shapes in order and look at the edges and the sizes. This is the time to trim any slightly skewed pieces. (Though remember, sometimes a rugged edge is very nice, so don't be too critical of imperfection.) Once you're satisfied, mark the sides on which you'll be applying glue, remembering that any time you glue a smaller piece to a larger one, you want to apply the glue to the smaller piece. Drizzle glue onto the first shape, use a scraper to scrape out a thin, even layer of glue, position the piece on top of the next one, and press them together (photos 11 through 13). If glue seeps out of the edges, clean it up at this point, then use a thinner layer of glue for the next two pieces. Continue to layer and glue. Layering is most successful when you use a glue that doesn't

set too quickly, one that allows you time to play with placement.

For tall projects such as the Vase Rubenesque, page 28, you can layer five or so pieces, then use a stack of heavy books to press the layers together. While those pieces are pressing, start on the next section. When the piece is com-

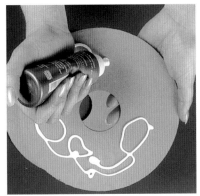
PHOTO 11

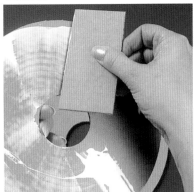
PHOTO 12

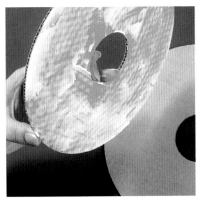
PHOTO 13

plete, pull out your home library's biggest books and press it overnight. Be sure to pay attention to the type of impression your books will leave. A flat book cover leaves a flat impression; a textured book jacket or edge may leave an unwanted texture.

LEAVING YOUR MARK

Here we go out on a cardboard limb to borrow a technique from our cousins the paper crafters: embossing. Pliable single-face and wave-flute cardboards offer endless options for a variety of embossing techniques.

Feed your board through a patterned embosser (or two!), and you can personalize all kinds of patterns. Or, send your cardboard through a pasta machine to emboss it with dimensional objects such as charms or coins. You can also hand emboss with trinkets and charms. Place the charm face up on your work surface, place a piece of single face, fluted side down, on top of it, and rub your bone folder over the object until you can see the image come through on the back of the paper. If your cardboard features fairly soft flutes and you're willing to apply some foot pressure, you can even use rubber stamps to create clear imprints. Large flat shapes work best.

With any embossed image, you can add a slight dusting of colored chalk to accentuate the raised areas. You can also use

CREATING DETAILED IMPRESSIONS WITH CHARMS

sandpaper to wear away the raised areas, giving colored cardboards a weathered look.

CRUSHING

Crushing reduces the size of the flutes of a piece of cardboard, making it easier to shape it and create items such as the flowers and leaves of the Cardboard

WITH A BIT OF PRESSURE, EVEN A STANDARD RUBBER STAMP CAN PRINT A PATTERN ON CARDBOARD.

Bouquet, page 70. It's also necessary to crush some of the more decorative boards, so they won't tear when you fold or curl them. Use either your bone folder's flat head or its side to crush small areas. Apply even pressure on the surface of your board until it's smushed evenly. (You don't want to leave smush lines.) Be careful when you crush the surface of decorative-flute boards; some of the top papers are delicate.

ROLLIN', ROLLIN', ROLLIN'

The following rolling techniques are the cardboard version of quilling or paper bead assembly. You can cut decorative cardboards into strips of various lengths and widths, then roll them to create shapes ranging from perfectly round to oblong. Because of its parallel flutes, single-face cardboard rolls easily. Wave flute and other decorative-flute boards must be crushed before you roll them. Whichever you use, you'll end up with rolls

that are strong enough to serve as structural accents, from drawer pulls to cabinet feet.

Here are the basic rolling steps:

1. Start by cutting out your cardboard strip, seaming several pieces together, if necessary, to get the strip length you need.

2. Crush your board if you're working with something other than single face, and preroll the strip in the direction you want it to go. Prerolling ensures that the core of the roll will be tight.

3. Apply glue to what will be the inside end or core of the roll. Roll the core, and hold the rolled core until the glue sets. Photo 14 shows two different ways to roll the core of a strip of single face, one with the flutes facing out and the other with the flutes facing in.

4. Add a line of glue down the center of the strip, and continue rolling to the very end. Clean up any glue up that squeezes out during the rolling.

5. Photo 15 shows two ways to finish a roll. One is to simply glue

PHOTO 14

down the end (see the roll on the right). The other is to strip off the last flutes and affix the backing over the previous layer of flutes.

PHOTO 15

Because I know of no official names for cardboard rolls, I've created some of my own to describe the rolls we'll be adding to projects throughout the book.

Floutist Roll

Roll single-face board with the flutes facing *out*, giving your roll a ridged texture, and you've got a Flou*t*ist.

Jelly Roll-Up

With a jelly roll, the good stuff is on the inside. With a Jelly Roll-Up, that's where the flutes of the single-face cardboard are. The smooth surface on the outside of this roll is perfect for adding attachments, such as the petals of a flower (see the Mum's the Word project, page 76).

Rolli-O

A Rolli-O is a variation of either a Floutist Roll or a Jelly Roll-Up. It features an open "O" at the core. Start the roll around a dowel, your finger, or anything that

gives the center of your roll the diameter you want.

Pot Scrubber Roll

It's a silly name, but it's apt. Don't you think the cardboard versions look like the real thing? Make shallow slits along one or both of the long edges of your starting strip to create little tabs. Preroll your strip. Then, as you glue, keep smashing the tabs flat. When you finish, you can fluff them out.

Nice Hat Roll

This roll makes a fashion statement with its spiraling peak. You can achieve it in either of two ways. One is to start with a straight strip of single face, and push the core up as you roll. Glue that sets slowly is a must with this method. The other is to use a strip that is wide at the core and narrows gradually as it extends to the end. The more gradual the narrowing, the rounder the top of your roll.

Rolly Top

This is just a roll with a decorative cap. Lay your completed roll

down on a piece of cardboard, and trace and cut a circular cover. Precut circles can define the roll diameter for consistent-sized rolls. Just roll to fit the cap.

Hard Roll

As the name suggests, this roll is a bit more difficult than the others. That's because it's created with standard cardboard (with paper on both sides of the flutes) rather than single-face board. Crushing and prerolling are essential; they make the cardboard pliable enough to be glued into a roll. Hard rolls make very sturdy supports.

Fold-a-Roll

To create this bulkier roll, with clean rather than raw edges, score and fold in the outer edges of your starting strip before you roll. This roll allows you to keep your colors consistent when your board has both colored and plain sides.

Now that you've got the basics you need to begin, peruse the book's projects and choose one that inspires you. The spirit of creativity awaits your call. Dive in. Everything is possible.

CHAPTER TWO

THE BOARD WALK

As the saying goes, you have to learn to walk before you run. Hence, The Boardwalk, a chapter of starter projects that incorporate the most basic steps in cutting and folding cardboard. To keep it exciting, I've tossed in some design twists that make the path more adventurous, but the road is yours to choose. And the results? Simply spectacular.

Vase
Rubenesque

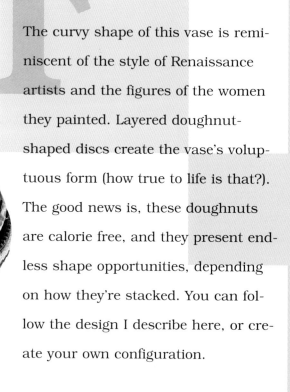

T

The curvy shape of this vase is reminiscent of the style of Renaissance artists and the figures of the women they painted. Layered doughnut-shaped discs create the vase's voluptuous form (how true to life is that?). The good news is, these doughnuts are calorie free, and they present endless shape opportunities, depending on how they're stacked. You can follow the design I describe here, or create your own configuration.

PREP

1. First, you need to cut the 130 circles that will form your vase, using the Circles to Cut list, page 30, as a guide. Don't be frightened by the number. A mat cutter makes this prep step a breeze. To create the vase's curvaceous shape, your circles need to first increase in size (from the mouth of the vase to the middle), then decrease (from the middle of the vase to the bottom), and then increase again to form the base. Cut your circles in order. As you cut, write the layer number on each circle, close to the center. The numbers will be hidden once you glue your circles together, but while you're cutting they'll help reduce the trauma of trying to remember what you've already cut.

2. When you finish, stack your circles in order (with #1 at the top) to see how the vase fits together. If you cut your circles with a mat cutter, when you get to layer #31 (which falls in the middle of the vase), flip your board over, so the beveled edges flow downward. You should also flip your board at layer #31 if your cardboard has a slight color difference on one side, or your color consistency won't be the same for the whole vase.

3. Mark the center of each circle. At each mark, cut a small circle; the circles will form a central column in the vase for holding a bouquet. I made my circles 2 inches in diameter, but you can cut yours wider if you wish. (Note: the two base pieces [layers 64 and 65] don't need center circles.) A mat cutter may not cut circles as small as the ones you need for your central column. If not,

you might decide that squares or triangles are easier; both shapes make fine central columns. Another option is to employ your circle paper cutter. Make a groove with its blade, then cut the rest of the circle out with a craft knife. (Here's where that rereading pays off. How do you cut a curve? Go to page 19.).

4. Stack your circles back in order, then flip the stack over, so the base is on the top of the stack.

ASSEMBLY

1. Look at your stack and notice where the flutes are wavy and where they're straight. Depending on the look you want, align the fluting patterns so they're vertical or so they wrap in a spiral fashion around the vase.

2. Glue, layer, and press the circles together one by one. (You did your rereading, right? No? Then go straight to Stick and Stack, page 23, if you need a refresher on gluing layers together.)

Assembly Tips:

■ When gluing, always apply the glue to the smaller of the surfaces being joined—it's logical if you think about it!

■ As I glued, I centered the circles by eye, matching the center column holes. If you don't cut out a center column through all your vase's layers, you can align the centers by sticking a straight pin through the center of one circle and then into the center of several adjoining layers.

MATERIALS
. . . .

25 sheets each of black, cream, and green wave-flute cardboard, 8 ½ x 11 inches (Your best bet for decorative board in these quantities is a store that sells scrapbooking supplies.)

Craft glue

TOOLS
. . . .

Circle mat cutter or paper circle cutter (You could also use a compass and a craft knife.)

Scraper

Craft knife

Big heavy books for pressing

SUGGESTED REREADING
. . . .

Cutting, page 19

Stick and Stack, page 23

FOR A MORE MINIMALIST VASE, USE KRAFT-COLORED B-FLUTE CARDBOARD RATHER THAN COLORED, DECORATIVE-FLUTE BOARD. BECAUSE IT'S THICKER, YOU NEED TO CUT ONLY 65 CIRCLES (ONE CIRCLE PER LAYER) OF B FLUTE TO MAKE THE VASE.

CIRCLES TO CUT

LAYER #	COLOR	DIAMET
(Cut 2 per layer)		
1."	green	3 ½"
2.	white	3 ⅝"
3.	black	3 ¾"
4.	green	3 ⅞"
5.	white	4"
6.	black	4 ⅛"
7.	green	4 ¼"
8.	white	4 ⅜"
9.	black	4 ½"
10.	green	4 ⅝"
11.	white	4 ¾"
12.	black	4 ⅞"
13.	green	5"
14.	white	5 ⅛"
15.	black	5 ¼"
16.	green	5 ⅜"
17.	white	5 ½"
18.	black	5 ⅝"
19.	green	5 ¾"
20.	white	5 ⅞"
21	black	6"
22.	green	6 ⅛"
23.	white	6 ¼"
24.	black	6 ⅜"
25.	green	6 ½"
26.	white	6 ⅝"
27.	black	6 ¾"
28.	green	6 ⅞"
29.	white	6 ⅞"
30.	green	6 ⅞"
31.	black	6 ¾"
32.	white	6 ⅝"

LAYER #	COLOR	DIAMETER
33.	green	6 ½"
34.	black	6 ⅜"
35.	white	6 ¼"
36.	green	6 ⅛"
37.	black	6"
38.	white	5 ⅞"
39.	green	5 ¾"
40.	black	5 ⅝"
41.	white	5 ½"
42.	green	5 ⅜"
43.	black	5 ¼"
44.	white	5 ⅛"
45.	green	5"
46.	black	4 ⅞"
47.	white	4 ¾"
48.	green	4 ⅝"
49.	black	4 ½"
50.	white	4 ⅜"
51.	green	4 ¼"
52.	black	4 ⅛"
53.	white	4"
54.	green	3 ⅞"
55.	black	3 ¾"
56.	white	3 ⅝"
57.	green	3 ½"
58.	black	3 ⅜"
59.	white	3 ¼"
60.	green	3 ⅛"
61.	black	3 ⅛"
62.	white	3"
63.	green	3"
64.	black	5"
65.	black	5 ⅛"

Metric Equivalents

⅛"	3 mm
½"	1.3 cm
2"	5 cm
3"	7.6 cm
3⅛"	7.9 cm
3¼"	8.2 cm
3⅜"	8.6 cm
3½"	8.9 cm
3⅝"	9.2 cm
3¾"	9.5 cm
3⅞"	9.8 cm
4"	10.2 cm
4⅛"	10.5 cm
4¼"	10.8 cm
4⅜"	11.2 cm
4½"	11.4 cm
4⅝"	11.8 cm
4¾"	12.1 cm
4⅞"	12.4 cm
5"	12.7 cm
5⅛"	13 cm
5¼"	13.3 cm
5⅜"	13.7 cm
5½"	14 cm
5⅝"	14.3 cm
5¾"	14.6 cm
5⅞"	14.9 cm
6"	15.2 cm
6⅛"	15.5 cm
6¼"	15.8 cm
6⅜"	16.2 cm
6½"	16.5 cm
6⅝"	16.8 cm
6¾"	17.1 cm
6⅞"	17.4 cm
8½"	21.6 cm
11"	27.9 cm

DIVING BOARD

■ The shape of the vase I chose is very classic. If you want something different, browse through fashion and home decorating magazines to gather ideas, then design a vase shape of your own. Or, transform the Vase Rubenesque design into a Grecian urn by adding handles. Simply sketch a basic handle shape (a half circle is common), cut and glue enough layers of the shape to give the handles substance, and glue the finished handles to the sides of the vase.

■ Try layering a variety of free-form shapes rather than circles. They don't require precision cuts or perfect centering. If you can cut it, try it!

■ Real flowers and water in a cardboard vase? Yes, and here's the trick. When you make your center column, measure it to fit a test tube, cigar container, or film canister. Fill the removable container with water, then insert it in the column.

■ Travel ahead to page 70 for instructions on making a beautiful bouquet of flowers for your vase that will last and last (no water necessary)—a real joy for those of us burdened with botanical brown thumbs.

■ Stack but don't glue your layers, then pencil a design, maybe triangles or diamonds, on the edges. Layer by layer, notch out the design anywhere from ⅛ to ½ inch deep. Ta-da! An inlaid pattern. Go another step, and inlay color. Sketch your design first on tracing paper, then transfer it to your vase layers and to the inlay material, such as single-face or wave-flute cardboard. Just remember, the curves in the vase will make it necessary to snip and ease the inlays into the recessed frames.

InVerse
Temple Bowl

The second project in our Boardwalk series reads like poetry—repeating stanzas of various-sized flutes and colored boards become the cascading tiers of a bowl. Aah, I know it's only cardboard, but if we think outside the box, it can seem to be so much more. A steady craft knife will be your main tool for making this simple ode to the artistry of cardboard.

PREP

1. Out of each of your seven 17-inch squares, use the craft knife to cut 12-inch squares, with all of the sides cut on a 45° angle to the flutes. Then, out of the 12-inch squares, cut 10-inch, 8-inch, 6-inch, and 4-inch squares (see figure 1). Don't stress if, in cutting out the smaller squares, you cut into the inner edges of the larger squares. Those inner edges (except for the ones on the top layer of B flute) will be hidden when you layer the pieces. If you get "furry flutes" on the edges of the cardboard pieces,

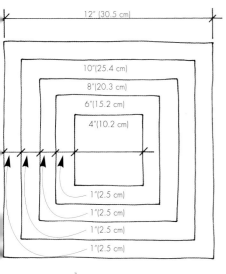

Fig. 1

you can smooth them: trim the fuzz with small scissors, then dab glue on a reduced-size cotton swab (see the Tool Tip) and insert it into the flutes and twirl it.

2. On the back of the 4-inch, 6-inch, and 8-inch squares of C flute, mark the center points on all four sides. Then, mark ¼ inch on either side of each center line. The marks will serve as glue guidelines for adding the base supports.

3. Transfer or lay out copies of the base pattern onto the twelve 4 x 3⅜-inch pieces, and cut them out. (You need three pieces for each of the four supports.)

ASSEMBLY

1. Layer and glue together all of the same-size squares (all of the 12-inch squares, all of the 10-inch squares, and so on), referring to figure 2 for the color sequence.

2. Layer and glue four sets of three base pieces, making four base supports.

3. You make the tiers of the bowl by reassembling the glued square sets, stacking the larger sets on top of the smaller ones. Start by rubbing glue around the edge of the top B-flute layer of the 4-inch set of squares, which becomes the bowl's bottom tier. Press it to the bottom C-flute layer of the 6-inch set. Check to make sure you've positioned the bottom square evenly. Add all the other square sets in the same way.

4. You'll notice that the notches on one side of each base support form three "steps." Squeeze a glue line onto these three steps on each of the four base supports, and adhere the supports to the assembled bowl.

MATERIALS
· ·

Inverse Temple Bowl pattern, page 117

3 squares of wave flute, 17 x 17 inches, in light green, peach, and cream

1 square of B flute, 17 x 17 inches, in kraft

1 square of E flute, 17 x 17 inches, in kraft

2 squares of C flute, 17 x 17 inches, in kraft

12 pieces of C flute, 4 x 3⅜ inches, in kraft

Craft glue

TOOLS
· ·

Cutting mat

Metal ruler or T-square

Right triangle

Craft knife and sharp blades

Scraper

Big heavy books for pressing

SUGGESTED REREADING
· ·

Be², page 17

Cutting, page 19

Stick and Stack, page 23

33

Use the center marks you made on the squares as guides.

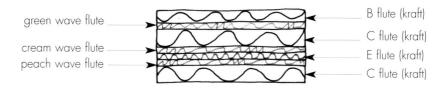

green wave flute	B flute (kraft)
cream wave flute	C flute (kraft)
peach wave flute	E flute (kraft)
	C flute (kraft)

Fig.2

Cutting Tip:

To prevent "fuzzy flutes" (or, as I also call them, "hairy scary edges"), use sharp, sharp blades in your craft knife. A three-step cutting process also helps "de-fray" the situation. Run the blade over the cutting line, cutting through the top layer, slice again to go through the fluting, then slice a third time to cut completely through.

Tool Tip:

To make a reduced-size cotton swab (good for dabbing glue on "fuzzy flutes"), pull off a small piece of cotton from the top of the swab and then tightly wind the remaining cotton back around the tip of the swab.

Pattern Pause:

If you change the number of layers in the square sets that make up your bowl, you'll need to change the step height on your base supports accordingly. The step height on the base support pattern provided here is ⅝ inch.

Metric Equivalents

¼"	6m
⅝"	1.6 c
3⅜"	8.6 c
4"	10.2 c
6"	15.2 c
8"	20.3 c
10"	25.4 c
12"	30.5 c
17"	43.2

DIVING BOARD

■ Don't stop here. Browse through books on antiques or ancient pottery for additional bowl shape inspirations. Or treat yourself to an art magazine from another country—you'll love the new perspective. Your research will give you an idea of the shapes of things past and the shapes of things to come.

■ Reverse the inverse process and make a lid for your bowl by cutting and gluing a complementary set of tiers. Add a decorative Floutist Roll as a knob (see page 25) to lift the lid.

■ Forget the base supports and make a hanging bowl. Weave four strands of ribbon in between the layers, from the small center bottom square out, using center guidelines. Glue the ribbons down to secure them. You'll need about 3 yards (2.7 m) of ribbon cut into even lengths for the bowl described here. When you're finished weaving, tie together all four ribbons over the center of the largest tier.

■ Shed some light on your bowl. Weave ribbons through the tiers, as described above, leaving an inch between each tier. Doing so creates a collapsible form which, when turned upside down, becomes a lamp shade or lantern. You can anchor a light fixture in the center square.

■ Delve into your childhood: Remember crayons? Pick out your favorite colors and scribble thickly along the edges of your bowl's tiers. Do zigzags or polka dots.

■ Bead your bowl. Cover the edges of your bowl's tiers with glue, then smother the glued spots with beads. There are also wonderful beaded fringes on the market that would look smashing.

■ In a more traditional mode, decoupage the inside of your bowl with ancient Grecian or sepia images. If you're going with this approach, you might want to change the colors in your tiers to gold, sepia, or black.

Punch
& Jewelry

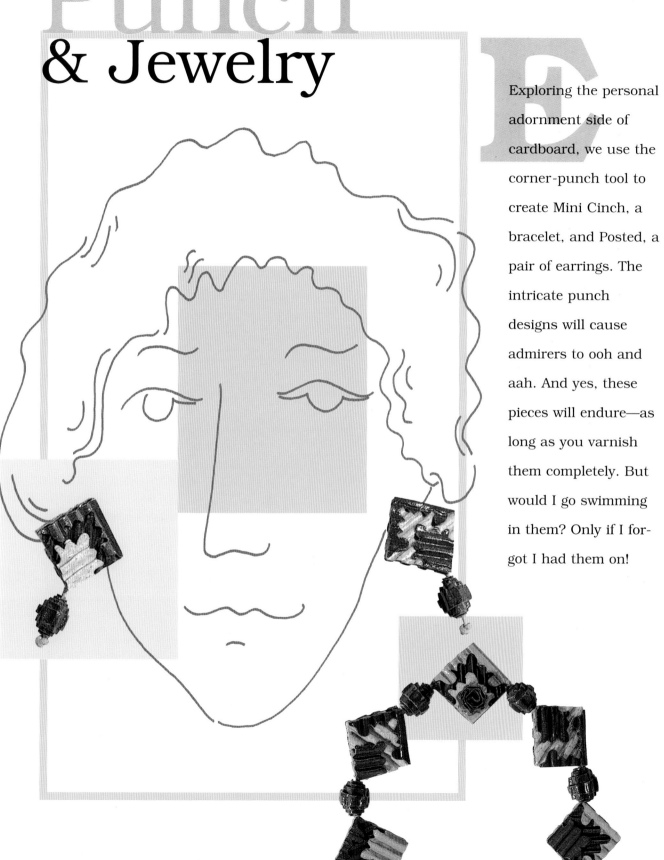

Exploring the personal adornment side of cardboard, we use the corner-punch tool to create Mini Cinch, a bracelet, and Posted, a pair of earrings. The intricate punch designs will cause admirers to ooh and aah. And yes, these pieces will endure—as long as you varnish them completely. But would I go swimming in them? Only if I forgot I had them on!

MATERIALS

Punch & Jewelry pattern, page 117

4 sheets of single-face cardboard, 8 ½ x 11 inches, in kraft, oatmeal, green, and burgundy

Tape

Craft glue

Length of ⅛-inch natural leather cord

U.V. varnish

Earring posts and backs (sold at bead and craft stores)

TOOLS

Cutting mat

Metal ruler or T-square

Craft knife

Corner punch

Scissors

⅛-inch hole punch

SUGGESTED REREADING

Metric Equivalents

⅛"	3 m
1¹⁄₁₆"	1.7 c
1"	2.5 c
8½"	21.6 c
11"	27.9 c
11¼"	28.5

Mini Cinch

PREP

1. Using the craft knife, cut out 10 squares measuring ¹¹⁄₁₆ inch, five in oatmeal and five in burgundy, with all of the sides cut on a 45° angle to the board's flutes.

2. Punch out two corner-punch sets in green, two in kraft, and one in oatmeal. Discard the squares, but keep the punched-out shapes for charm assembly.

3. Referring to photos 1 and 2, trim out the "crowns" of the punched shapes, cutting peaks at the bottoms. The peaks will sit in the corner of the front of the charms.

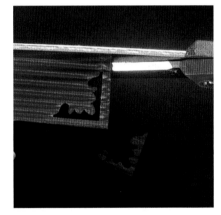

PHOTO 1

4. Assemble the fronts of the charms (the squares you cut in step 1) by placing the trimmed crowns onto two oatmeal and three burgundy squares (use the photo as a guide). Glue the pieces together.

5. Use the bead pattern on page 117 to cut out five burgundy bead strips. Perform a Floutist Roll on each strip. (This is not a gymnastic move, so you may want to refer

back to the Rollin', Rollin', Rollin' section, page 24, to refresh your memory on Floutist Rolls.)

6. Cut a length of leather cord for the base of the bracelet. You want it long enough that the bracelet will slide easily on and off your wrist, but not so long that it will slip off (mine is 11¼ inches).

ASSEMBLY

1. Fold the cord in half and mark the center. Spread glue on the back of a plain oatmeal square. Place the center of the cord on the square's diagonal. Align one of the decorated burgundy squares on top of the oatmeal square, and press, sandwiching the cord between the layers (refer to the project photo for front pattern selection if you want the order of your charms to match mine). Slide a bead onto the cord on either side of the center charm.

2. Attach decorated oatmeal squares for the next two charms, using burgundy squares as backings. String on two more beads, then attach the last two burgundy charms, using oatmeal backs.

PHOTO 2

3. Add a drop of glue into both threading holes of the last bead. Insert the two ends of the cording to close the bracelet. Let it set.

4. Optional: Glue a loose burgundy rosette onto the center charm. (Use half the height and width of the bead pattern, and roll a loose Floutist Roll to create your rosette.)

5. Varnish, varnish, varnish.

Posted

PREP

1. Cut out squares the same size as those you cut in Prep step 1 for the bracelet: two in burgundy and two in oatmeal. In addition, create three corner-punch squares, one in green, one in burgundy, and one in oatmeal. Glue together the charm faces, using the project photo as a guide. (Yes, my earrings are purposely mismatched; feel free to make yours a matching set.)

2. Cut out two bead strips in burgundy, and create two Floutist Rolls.

3. Pull a knot in a length of cord. On one end, clip very close to the knot and seal the knot with glue. On the other end, cut the cord 1 inch above the knot. Repeat this process with another length of cord.

4. Punch a ⅛-inch hole in the center of one burgundy and one oatmeal square.

ASSEMBLY

1. Thread a bead onto the cording.

2. Insert one of the posts through the hole of one of the backing squares, coming through to the back of the square.

3. Dab glue onto the back of one of the charms. Center the cording and bead droplet over the bottom corner of the backing square, leaving wiggle room for the bead. Align the charm and the backing square, and seal them together with glue (see figure 1).

4. Repeat steps 1 through 3 to create your second earring.

5. Varnish, and you are ready to be adorned with paper.

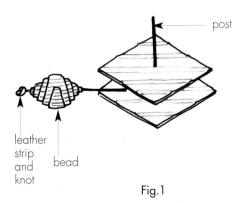

post

leather strip and knot

bead

Fig.1

DIVING BOARD

With its natural and earthy appeal, cardboard jewelry vies for attention alongside expensive metals and stones. It's sturdy yet delicate—a delightful dichotomy—and admirers will be amazed when they find out what your jewels are made from. With all the hole punches and decorative-edge scissors now on the market, creating imaginative designs is simple. The hardest part is choosing your combination of colors, shapes, punches, and cuts.

■ Don't forget about the option of manipulating cardboard: rolling, crushing, and layering (refer back to the Board Basics chapter, page 7). Each technique can add a unique look to your accessories.

■ Think beads. Glass beads in teeny tiny sizes, ceramic beads in dynamic colors, flashy beads from different metals. Mix your boards and beads to accent your look.

■ Get wired! Wire now comes in all thicknesses and colors. Punch out a design and fill in the slits and slots with wire clippings or coils. Connect your cardboard charms with wire wiggles. I could go on, but this is the fun part, so I'll leave you to it.

E-Zeemoney

E-commerce, E-mail, E-eeeek! You'll be
happy to know the "E" in this project title stands
for things more basic and tangible: E-flute single-face cardboard (it's the "fabric" of the
wallet), embossing (the decorative technique we'll use), and easy (as in the best kind
of project to approach). No virtual reality here, just good old-fashioned cutting and
folding—taking cardboard into new dimensions.

MATERIALS

E-Zeemoney patterns, page 118

Several sheets of single-face E-flute cardboard, 11½ x 11½ inches, in a color or colors of your choice

Tape

Craft glue (Substitute craft cement if you're using metallic cardboard in place of one of the colors specified.)

Decorative tissue or paper (optional)

Decoupage glue (optional)

Decorative snap fasteners (pronged), ⁷⁄₁₆-inch size

Different-shaped paper clips or formed wire coils

Varnish

TOOLS

Cutting mat

Craft knife or scissors

Metal ruler or T-square

Bone folder

Decorative-edge scissors (optional)

Hole punches: circles and other decorative styles you like (optional)

SUGGESTED REREADING

Scoring, page 19

Leaving Your Mark, page 23

40

Metric Equivalents

⁷⁄₁₆"	1.1 cm
¾"	1.9 cm
11½"	29.2 cm

PREP

1. Enlarge the patterns for the wallet and the coin case, page 118, and transfer them each to the cardboard. Note the direction of the flutes indicated on the patterns, and square the patterns to the flutes on the actual cardboard (you can make the pieces the same or different colors). Cut out both pieces.

2. On both pieces, score all the fold lines that don't run parallel to the flutes. Roll the parallel flutes on the spine of the wallet and the coin case flap. This breaks the stiffness of the boards. They should roll freely.

Pattern Pause:

By cutting off the wallet's credit card flap (portion E), you can introduce a third color into your wallet design. Trace this portion onto a different color of cardboard, adding a ¾-inch strip to the end where you made the cut. To reattach the new portion E, glue the added strip to the body of the wallet. Our wallet in primary colors demonstrates this option.

ASSEMBLY

1. Decorate your wallet piece. You can emboss it with various charms and images in a pattern of your choice, and/or punch holes and refill them with contrasting colors of cardboard.

2. If you want to line your wallet with lightweight tissue or paper, now is the time. You don't need to cut another pattern. Simply decoupage a sheet of paper to the inside of the wallet and coin case, then trim off the excess paper.

3. Rescore all the folds on both pieces. Do so gently, with the side of the bone folder rather than the end, so you don't tear the liner.

4. Refer to figure 1 for assembling the wallet body. Fold up sides A and B, lining to lining. Apply glue to the lining side of strip C, and secure it to the edge of side B. Fold up center flap D (see pattern), dab it with glue, and press it in place to the inside of the spine. This closes the bottom fold while adding strength to a vulnerable joint. Fold over piece

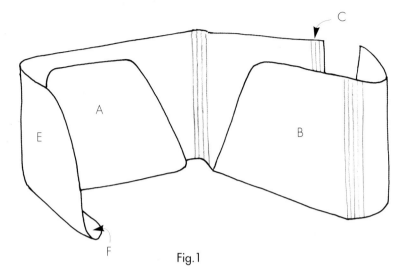

Fig. 1

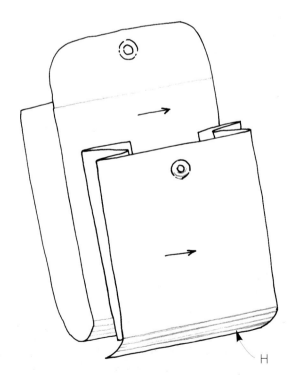

Fig. 2

E (the credit card flap). Smudge glue onto the lining side of piece F, and roll it over to the front side of the wallet.

5. Refer to figure 2 for attaching the coin case to the wallet body. Position the coin case sides (the pieces marked G on the pattern) on the outside of wallet piece C, and align the sides. Fold over the coin case flap, and mark where the snap closure will go. Run glue down the G flaps, align them again, then attach them to piece C, holding them in place until the bond sets. Dab flap H with glue, fold it over, and seal it onto the center spine of the folded wallet, closing the bottom of the coin case.

7. Varnish. Let everything set before you apply the snaps, following the manufacturer's instructions.

DIVING BOARD

■ Deposit some bleach and withdraw some color. Splatters of bleach will remove the color on your cardboard, creating a snowflake-like print. Be very careful with bleach and read the precautionary labels. If you use too much, you may remove your cardboard's flutes!

■ Blow through a straw into a solution of dish-washing liquid and paint, and you create a colored foam you can use to pull a cardboard print of bubbles. Get wild, and layer several colors of bubbles onto your cardboard.

■ For a wallet with a more masculine look, leave off the coin case, and trim the coin case cover flap to roll over to the front. Glue it down to close the end of the wallet.

■ Consider the potentially marvelous results of embossing—and embossing mistakes. While I was working on my wallets, my son Tyler accidentally stepped on one of the sheets of cardboard I had lying on the floor. What became of the board? Look at the green wallet (below). The embossing tool for this one was Tyler's misplaced shoe. Go ahead and experiment with all kinds of instruments and leave your own original mark.

Whirlwined

H

Here's a new twist on the traditional wine rack. To make it, we switch the layering process used in earlier projects. Instead of stacking horizontal layers of cardboard, we run them vertically. We also alternate fluted edges with the split edges of parallel-flute cardboard to make the pattern of the piece more interesting. Finally, we imbed the cardboard with wire to keep the "swirl" in the rack's curl. When you're finished, you've got the perfect place to keep bottles of wine or water (imported, of course) until you're ready to toast yourself on a job well done.

MATERIALS

CARDBOARD FOR RACK (ALL KRAFT B FLUTE)

- 8 pieces, 9 x 7 inches
- 8 pieces, 7 x 9 inches
- 6 pieces, 5⅞ x 7 inches
- 6 pieces, 7 x 5⅞ inches
- 6 pieces, 4⅝ x 7 inches
- 6 pieces, 7 x 4⅝ inches

When you cut these pieces, you want the flutes of the cardboard to run in the direction of the first measurement number. For example, on the 9 x 7-inch pieces, the fluting would run parallel to the 9-inch edge.

OTHER MATERIALS

Whirlwined patterns, page 119

Sheet of red single flute, 8½ x 11 inches

Craft cement

Craft glue

3 wire strips, 20 gauge, 24 inches long

TOOLS

Cutting mat

Craft knife

Metal ruler or T-square

Bone folder

Popsicle stick (optional)

Wire clippers (or scissors)

Scraper

A few books

SUGGESTED REREADING

Cutting, page 19

Stick and Stack, page 23

WHAT TO CUT

Use the patterns on page 119 to cut the following pieces.

DESCRIPTION	QTY	MATERIAL
Full swirl panel	4	9 x 7-inch blanks
Full swirl panel	4	7 x 9-inch blanks
Uneven points panel	6	⅝ x 7-inch blanks
Uneven points pane	6	7 x 4 ⅝-inch blanks
Even points panel	6	5⅞ x 7-inch blanks
Even points panel	6	7 x 5⅞-inch blanks
Loose swirl panel	4	9 x 7-inch blanks
Loose swirl panel	4	7 x 9-inch blanks

Prep

1. Use the patterns to cut all the panels.

2. To see how the rack comes together, stack your panels in the following order: 8 full swirl panels, 6 uneven points panels, 12 even points panels, 6 flipped-over uneven points panels, 8 loose swirl panels. Alternate the fluting pattern as you stack, aligning the bottom corners of the pieces. Flipping over the second set of uneven points panels gives you a graduated point height.

3. In step 4, you'll embed wire in the second, fourth, and sixth full swirl panels, to help hold the front swirls' curls. To create a bed for the wire, run your craft knife through the first layer of paper on the top of each cardboard panel, and cut a groove starting at the center of the swirl to the top edge of the swirl (see figure 1). Run your bone folder into the grooves you've cut.

4. Insert wire into the slotted grooves on each panel, starting at the center of the full swirl and shaping the wire as you go. Embed the wire into the groove with your bone folder. If you're not able to embed the wire securely, dab craft cement under the wire and hold it in place with the end of a Popsicle stick until it sets. Clip the wire at the end of the groove.

5. Restack the panels.

6. Cut a variety of triangular shapes from the red single flute.

Prep Alternative:

If you don't want the edges of your rack to feature alternating flute

Metric Equivalents

2"	5 cm
3"	7.6 cm
4⅝"	11.8 cm
5⅞"	14.9 cm
7"	17.8 cm
8½"	21.6 cm
9"	22.9 cm
11"	27.9 cm
24"	61 cm

directions, you can cut all your full swirl and loose swirl panels out of blank board cut in the same way (cut 16 9 x 7-inch blanks, for example).

Cutting Tip:

Always use a sharp blade for curved cuts, and use the "sawing" method described in Cutting, page 19, to help with the tight curves in the full swirl. Trim pieces with small, curved scissors.

ASSEMBLY

1. Scrape a layer of glue on the first panel, and press the next panel

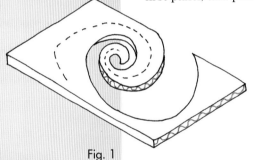

Fig. 1

on top of it. Continue to glue, stack, and press. Let the glue set overnight.

2. Gently stretch out the tip of the front swirl (where the neck of your bottle will rest). To avoid tearing the piece, you want to ease it out slowly. The best way is to insert a small stack of books between this portion and the rest of the swirl (your stack should measure about 2 to 3 inches). This is a gradual process; you'll need to leave the books in place overnight. Be sure to choose books that won't leave an impression in the board while they're stretching the swirl open.

3. Once the swirl is open, remove the books and apply the triangle appliqués, to create an additional sense of motion. Lay the triangles down randomly on your rack's surface in a pattern you like, then glue them down.

DIVING BOARD

■ Build a couple of Whirlwined racks and glue them together for a wine wall. If you alter the pattern, forgetting the swirl and making giant block-letter "U" shapes instead, you'll be able to stack an entire honeycomb of holders for your sweets of the vine.

■ Take lessons from our other layered projects and drop some color between the kraft layers. Use colored single-face cardboard to cover the interior edges of the full and loose swirls, creating a colored swirl. If you seam a rainbow of colors together, the swirl takes on a roller coaster motion.

■ Put a different spin on the project. Change the shape a bit by putting angles where the curves are. Or try mirror images of a different shape entirely—maybe a heart-shaped rack?

■ Wines have a distinctive flavor—why not a distinctive carrier? Add some pointed ears, Rolli-O feet (see page 25), and a tiny snout, and you've got a wine pig. Change the snout to a grill and the feet to wheels, and give your wine a real spin around the block. You could even give the Whirlwined a roof and build a house for an excellent housewarming gift.

CHAPTER THREE

A LEG UP

WE TOOK OUR FIRST STEPS IN CARDBOARD
DESIGN WITH THE BOARDWALK PROJECTS.
NOW, WE PICK UP THE PACE. TO HELP YOU
DO THAT, THE PROJECTS IN THIS CHAPTER
OFFER SOME SHORTCUTS, OR A PROVERBIAL
LEG UP. THEY REDUCE THE TIME YOU SPEND
MEASURING AND CUTTING YOUR BOARD, SO
YOU CAN MOVE MORE QUICKLY INTO BUILD-
ING AND EMBELLISHING. ONCE YOU GET
GOING, YOU'LL FIND YOUR UNDERSTANDING
OF DESIGN AND ASSEMBLY GROWING, ALLOW-
ING YOU TO INCORPORATE YOUR OWN CON-
CEPTS INTO THE PROJECTS, WHICH IS EXACTLY
THE IDEA. THESE PROJECTS ARE THE STEPPING
STONES TO YOUR CARDBOARD INDEPEND-
ENCE.

NOTE: IN A FEW OF THE PROJECTS IN THIS CHAPTER, WE OFFER
A LEG UP BY SUGGESTING PRECUT CARDBOARD PIECES YOU
CAN PURCHASE INSTEAD OF CUTTING YOUR OWN. ON PAGE
144, WE GIVE YOU ORDERING INFORMATION. IF YOU'RE A
FROM-SCRATCH PURIST AND YOU WANT TO MAKE THE PIECES
YOURSELF INSTEAD OF PURCHASING THEM, WE ALSO PROVIDE
YOU WITH INSTRUCTIONS FOR DOING SO.

No-Bake Boxes

I don't know about you, but I use my kitchen utensils for crafts much more than for cooking. As a result, I've come up with all kinds of appetizing ideas; the recipe for these decorative and gift boxes is one of my favorites. The secret ingredient? Cookie cutters. Go check. You must have some in your kitchen—or craft closet. They come in unlimited shapes, so you can make boxes with nearly any personality. Once you've got your base box, you can top it with beads, bows, or dried flowers, or even mix in some interesting fabric, and serve up a whole new look.

PREP

1. Trace the inside and the outside of the cookie cutter onto separate pieces of the cardboard for your lid and base. Cut them out. The inside (smaller) outline becomes the bottom of the box; the outside (larger) one defines the lid.

2. Determine the box's perimeter measurement by wrapping a piece of the single-face cardboard, fluting to the outside, around the lid.

3. Cut two strips of single face to match this perimeter measurement, one that's wide enough to create the height you want for your box and another that's wide enough to give you the height you want for the lip of your box's lid. If it's necessary to seam two pieces of the single-face cardboard together to create one piece that will wrap the entire perimeter, make the seamed piece wide enough that you can cut both strips from it.

4. Choose your filling—that is, whether to line the inside of the strips (which will make up the inside walls of your box) or to leave them plain. If you want to line them, use a lightweight decoupage glue to apply tissue or craft glue for other decorative papers.

5. If you don't want your box to have exposed cardboard tops and bottoms, cover both sides of the lid and base pieces with decorative paper. Glue the paper onto one side and let it dry. Trim around the perimeter. Do the same to the other side.

6. Decide on embellishments to decorate the top of your box and gather them or cut them out of various colors of single-face cardboard. You can cut out facial features for animal shapes, use dried flowers on round shapes...the options are endless.

Design Tip:

The more intricate the shape of the cookie cutter, the lower the height of the box will need to be for the sides to hold the shape. But be aware, with very intricate shapes, even if you work the folds and crease the detailed perimeters, the sides may not hold the shape. You can try embedding a horizontal wire in between the lining and the side, or running wires vertically in the flutes of the sides, but even these are not foolproof solutions. Your best bet is to choose cookie cutters with simple shapes.

MATERIALS

Small pieces of cardboard; any size flute will do (for box lid and base)

Sheets of E-flute single-face cardboard in a variety of colors

Decorative papers (for linings)

Cookie cutters

Craft glue

Decoupage glue (optional)

TOOLS

Cutting mat

Scissors or craft knife

Metal ruler or T-square

SUGGESTED REREADING

Seams Like a Winner, page 22

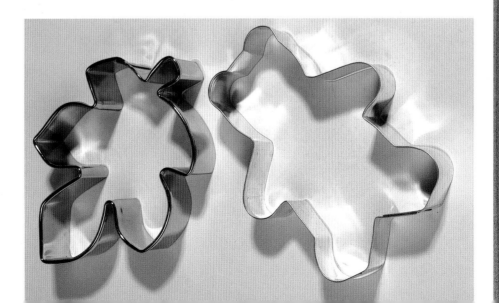

The same cookie cutter outlines you use to create box lids and bottoms can be your guides in making decorative lid covers and liners. I used a tracing of the outside of the teddy bear cookie cutter to design my bear's cloths. For the leaf box cover, I traced the outside of the cookie cutter onto ochre B-flute cardboard, then sliced through the shape to replicate the pattern of veins in a leaf and to reveal contrasting paper on the lid underneath. I also used drops of bleach to alter the color patterns on the B flute, making the piece look more like a fall leaf.

ASSEMBLY

1. Choose an inconspicuous place to start and end the wrapping of the side strip. Run a bead of glue an inch or two long around the edge of the box bottom. Leave the first three of the side flutes unglued, then position the side piece and hold it in place. Continue running beads of glue and pressing the side strip in place around the form.

2. When the ends meet, seam them together.

3. Repeat the process to attach the other side strip to the lid. Let both pieces dry.

4. Decorate the outside of your box with the embellishments you've chosen.

DIVING BOARD

■ Nesting cookie cutters can make a tower of boxes. Use them to cut actual cookies several sizes smaller than your box, bake them, and you've got a gift and matching gift box.

■ A false bottom can help the sides of your box hold the shape of a more detailed cookie cutter. Before you glue on the side strip, draw a line where you want the base to go. Follow this line when you attach the strip. You'll simply end up with a shallower interior.

■ Fancy decor is one coating of lightweight glue away. Find a glue that won't saturate and dissolve the flutes and can adhere lightweight papers together. When you apply the papers, the fluting transforms them into dimensional columns of rolling color. Beautiful wrapping paper and tissue are excellent for interiors or exteriors.

Make
a Stand

If you fancy the classic architecture of ancient Rome and Greece, if you marvel over the ingenuity it took to build those columns, then you'll really marvel at the ease of these. We take into consideration modern time constraints, so you *can* build your own bit of Rome in a day! Single-face cardboard makes an outstanding column body, complete with flutes that pose perfectly as carved grooves. A set of triple-thick cardboard circles provides the ready-to-wrap base, and square frames top it off. Together, they make it easy for you to make your own stand in decorating history.

MATERIALS

Make a Stand patterns, page 120

2 Boardering the Norm Frames*

2 inner circles from Ring-a-Ding Dings*

2 pieces of C-flute single-face cardboard, 1 measuring 23½ x 36 inches and 1 measuring 12 inches x 12 inches

Heavy-duty paper bag or kraft paper

Craft glue

*To cut down on your own prep, purchase these ready-to-go triple-layer pieces; ordering information appears on page 144. If you'd rather make your own, follow the first two Prep steps. You'll also need additional blank cardboard if you're making the pieces yourself: 6 squares of C flute, 9 x 9 inches, and 6 circles of C flute, 7¼ inches in diameter.

TOOLS

Scraper

Metal ruler at least 36 inches long

Cutting mat

Craft knife

SUGGESTED REREADING

Seams Like a Winner, page 22

Metric Equivalents

2⅝"	6.6 c
7¼"	18.4 c
9"	22.9 c
12"	30.5 c
23½"	59.7 c
36"	91.4

PREP

1. If you want to make your own two triple-layer squares (rather than ordering the Boardering the Norm Frames), begin with your six 9-inch squares of C flute. With the scraper, distribute an even layer of glue over one side of one square, and press it together with a second. Scrape another layer of glue over the second square, and press the third in place. Press the triple-layer square under books until the glue is dry. Repeat the process to create your second triple-layer square.

2. If you want to make your own two triple-layer circles (rather than ordering the Ring-a-Ding Dings), next you need your six C-flute circles measuring 7¼ inches in diameter. With the scraper, distribute an even layer of glue over one side of one circle, and press it together with a second. Scrape another layer of glue over the second circle, and press the third in place. Press the triple-layer circle under books until the glue is dry. Repeat the process to create your second triple-layer circle.

3. Find the center of each of the square frames by drawing diagonal lines from corner to corner. The center point is where all 4 lines meet. On each square, mark four points 2⅝ inches in toward the center from each corner.

4. On each square, lay down one of the circles, and line it up with the marks. Trace the circles.

5. Cover the unmarked sides of each square frame with a grocery bag or kraft paper. If you want something more than plain paper, you could cover the squares with doilies or with cutout and hole-punched decorative patterns.

6. Preroll your column to check your measurements and determine where to cut the piece. Roll the large C-flute band of single face around one of the circles, and cut the piece, along its 36-inch edge, where one or two flutes overlap the starting edge. Cut as close to the base of the ending flute as possible without opening the fluted edge. Cut the backing off the overlap flutes. Again, for a refresher, reread Seams Like a Winner, page 22.

7. Using the pattern on page 120, cut out four corner rolls and four corner details from the square of C flute single face.

ASSEMBLY

1. Run a line of glue along the top edge of the column band. Hold one of the circles in the center of the top edge, so the top of the circle is flush with the edge of the band. Bring the ends of the band up to meet each other, covering the entire edge of the circle in the process. Hold the edges together until the glue sets.

2. Run a line of glue along the edge of the other circle. Insert the circle into the open end of the column band, being careful of the glue and aligning the outer surface of the circle with the edges of the band. Press the pieces together until the band is securely in place.

3. Dab glue onto your fingertips and insert them to the seaming flap of the band. Slide them down to seam the edge, then press the edge

in place, creating a closed tube out of the column band. You can run a bone folder down the finished seam to conform the flutes of the column.

4. On both ends, cover the top of the circle with a layer of glue, and press the squares in place, following the pencil guides.

5. Shape the corner rolls by rolling the pieces. When you get the roll you like, glue the large end of the curl under the corners of the column's square frame. Dab glue onto the portion of the curl that rests on the main column. Glue on the corner details, using figure 1 as a guide.

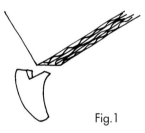

Fig.1

Assembly Tip:

If your corner curls don't touch your main column, you may have trouble keeping them curly. Cut a mirror image of each piece to be curled, then glue the two pieces together with a twist tie in between them. The wire in the tie will help the curls hold their shape.

DIVING BOARD

■ How about making your column a true ringer? Instead of finishing each end with a square frame, cut a pair of larger rings and use them. (If you order Ring-a-Ding Dings for this project, you can simply use both the inner circle and the outer ring that come with each set.)

■ If you top your column with a ring and a circle, as suggested above, inset the circle to create a recessed area on your column's top. When gluing on the top of your column band, glue around the bottom layer of your center circle. When you slide on the ring, it will sit above it. Fill the recess with trinkets you want to display and cover it in glass. Or, reverse the whole process and build up your column's top by gluing on a second triple-layer circle.

■ Mix up your design by trying a square base and a circle top or vice versa. Drape strands of ivy around it (jump ahead to see how cardboard ivy grows, page 73). Spray-paint your column white and distress it with sandpaper for a time-seasoned finish.

■ Use your columns as structural elements. Put two together, and top them with a piece of clear plastic sheeting. This makes a shelf or back-of-the-couch table. For added internal strength, you can embed the ends of a plywood dowel into each of a column's solid circles before you wrap the column's band around them.

Hall Light

W

We're slowly progressing through history, from ancient Greece (with the Make a Stand column, page 51) up to the Renaissance, updating classic looks with a combination of humor and style. Here, we bring some laughter into your halls by introducing the lighter side of fixturing: a jester wall sconce. The fun and folly begin with the same standard circles of cardboard used in other projects throughout the book—bet you never knew they could be this versatile!

PREP

1. If you want to make your own two sets of triple-layer rings and circles (rather than ordering the Ring-a-Ding Dings), cut circles measuring 7¼ inches in diameter out of the centers of the six C-flute circles. With the scraper, distribute even layers of glue and layer the outer rings and inner circles, creating two triple-layer versions of each. (You'll use only one of the triple-layer inner circles. Set the other aside for another project.)

Note: The manufactured Ring-a-Ding Dings are a standard ⅝ inches thick. If you create your own rings and circles, they may not match this thickness. If not, add another layer or two of cardboard until they do.

2. Divide one of the triple-layer rings into thirds and mark points. To create exact cut lines, use your measuring tape to mark points on the ring, each 5¾ inches from the other. Then, insert one of the solid circles inside the ring. Mark the exact center of the solid circle from that point. Use your ruler to draw lines from the center to each of the three points on the ring. This creates your three cut lines on the ring.

3. Cut the ring into the thirds you marked. Stack the three arcs. When you glue them later, they'll form the base of your sconce.

4. On the top arc of your stack, cut ⅝ inch off of each end. Mark the center of this arc with a notch, and make marks ⁵⁄₁₆ inch from either side of the notch. Cut slits on the ⁵⁄₁₆-inch marks, going through the first two layers of cardboard.

5. I have no idea what the floppy points on jester hats are actually called, so I've named these party horns. To make them, divide your other ring into thirds (points A, C, and E on figure 1). Then add three additional points (again, see figure 1). Mark two of the points, points B and D, on the ring's outside edge, 3⅜ inches from the original points A and C. Mark point F on the ring's inside edge, 3¾ inches from the point E.

6. Make arcs connecting these

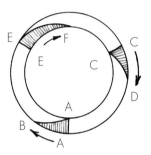

Fig. 1

points, as shown in figure 1. Cut out the three party horns. The larger horn will fit in the center slit you cut in the arced base in step 4. The matching party tooters will fit in the ⅝-inch recesses.

7. The blue and gold strips will serve as the sconce's front bands. Cut a random large pinking pattern on one long edge of the blue band, with the valleys going down no farther than 1 inch. Your first valley should hit 1¾ inches from the end of the strip. This point is where the band wraps around the sides of the sconce to the front.

8. Transfer a copy of the bell pattern on page 120 to each of the three gold single-face squares, and cut out the pieces. Slit the center of each piece, and punch holes on the end of each slit, following the lines on the pattern.

9. Work over the bell pieces to break the board's stiffness, then cement the ends of the four tips together. Keep working the shape while you're cementing to achieve a round bell (see figure 2).

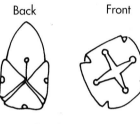

Back   Front

Fig. 2

10. To make a ledge for your sconce's light, you need to fit a portion of one of your circles into the arc that will serve as the bottom layer of the sconce's base. Fit the circle in place temporarily, mark a line where you need to cut it (see figure 3), and remove the circle and make the cut. If you want to extend the ledge, cut straight back from the base endpoints instead of across, and square off the back of the circle.

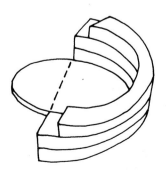

Fig. 3

11. Using the pattern on page 120, cut out three paper ears from the grocery bag or kraft paper. Fold your paper before cutting, and align the pattern on the fold, so you cut out a double image. The paper ears will connect to the backs of the party horns.

12. Time to dress those party horns in style. Apply glue to one side of each of the horns. Press the glued sides onto the purple wave flute. When the bond is dry, trim the pieces out. Glue the other sides of the arcs to green wave flute, and repeat the process. To conceal the raw edges in the middle of the horns, cut ⅝-inch strips of red wave flute, and glue them on.

Prep Tip:

If you're afraid to cut the pinking pattern on your blue band freehand, lightly pencil your design on the back of the band first. Be sure to erase your pencil lines with a clean eraser after cutting; the points your cuts create are supposed to curl forward slightly, so pencil marks and dirty eraser smudges would be visible.

Design Tip:

If you want to camouflage the bulges on the backs of the bells (where the four points meet), cover them with thin Floutist Rolls (see page 25), or glue on discs of gold single face.

ASSEMBLY

1. You don't need a milliner's touch to make this hat, just a methodical approach. Layer the base arcs together, remembering

that the top layer is the one with the center notch and the end cuts. The notch should face up.

2. Drop glue in the ⅝-inch spaces on the ends and onto the raw edges of the shortened top arc. Slide the two small party horns into place, green sides out and horns going forward (see figure 4). Hold the horns in place until the bond is secure.

3. With your bone folder, crush the center notch so the slot sits at an angle. The inside end of the slot should sit about ½ to ¾ inch lower than the outside end of the slot. Insert the large horn and glue it into place. The angled slot raises the horn tip so it sits higher than the others.

4. Attach one paper ear to the center horn by gluing the fold of the ear to the middle of the center horn. Glue down the bottom of the ear to the inside of the base arc. Attach the other two ears in the same way; they'll overlap the center ear. Trim the ears on the outside edge of the two outer horns, so the ears are flush with the horn edges.

5. Run the 9-inch strips of C flute down the center of the back of each horn, leaving three or four flutes dangling off the end of the pointed ends.

6. Get your cardboard jingles and jangle them at the end of the dangling strip. (In other words, glue the bells in place.)

Lighting Up Your Sconce:

You can use your cardboard sconce with a battery-operated light, a low-watt fixture, or a single bulb from a

56

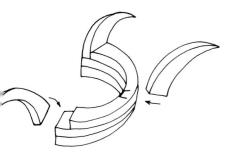

Fig. 4

Twist the ends of the loop together, and insert them into the middle layer of the cardboard arc.

Mounting Your Sconce:

Your sconce can sit happily on a shelf. Or, you can mount it with a small "L" bracket from a hardware store. Attach the bracket to the wall.

holiday strand. Simply puncture a hole in the sconce's ledge for the electrical cord, or skip the ledge and create a wire loop to cradle the bulb.

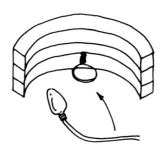

Create a wire loop to cradle the blub

DIVING BOARD

■ Create a Mardi Gras atmosphere year-round by hanging a series of sconces down the hall. Why not try a crown or hat made for a princess? Sheer papers and tissues cast unusual colors of light.

■ Here's the punch line: Decorative hole punches in your cardboard sconces make playful windows that twinkle in the dark.

■ Want a wizard of an idea? Punch moons and stars out of handmade papers fashioned in the shape of a cone on a cardboard, half-circle base.

■ How about storming the night with a Viking

Hangin' Around

O Once, many of us giggled at people who kept their holiday lights up all year long. Now, year-round strings of twinkling minilights are trendy, as long as your lights make a statement. We show you how to make the ultimate statement, with three different customized cardboard covers for standard strands of lights. The basic method for each light cover is the same. How you wrap and adorn them changes their look. The result: strings of one-of-a-kind lanterns you'll be proud to have hanging around for a while.

BASIC LIGHT COVERS

BASIC LIGHT COVERS

MATERIALS

2 sets of Ovalettes* (makes 6 lights)

Sheet of decorative cardboard for each light (any color or style of your choice)

Craft glue (Use craft cement if you're working with metallic cardboard.)

Strand of home decor or holiday bulbs with butterfly clips

*To cut down on your own prep, pur-chase these ready-to-go pieces; order-ing information appears on page 144. If you'd rather make your own Ovalettes, use the pattern on page 121 and follow the first Prep step. You'll also need some blank cardboard: 3 rectangles of C flute per lantern, 5 x 7 inches.

TOOLS

Cutting mat

Craft knife

Metal ruler

Scissors

Optional tools for decorating your wrap (stamps, hole punches, etc.)

SUGGESTED REREADING

Seams Like a Winner, page 22

Leaving Your Mark, page 23

PREP

1. If you want to make your own ovals (rather than ordering the Ovalettes), use the pattern, page 121, and cut three ovals per lantern out of the C-flute cardboard, then glue them together to create a triple-wall piece.

2. For each light cover, you need a basic cardboard wrap that is 4 inch-es wide x 13 ⅛ inches long. You'll likely need to seam together several pieces of cardboard to create a wrap that's long enough. If you're using board that can't be seamed, such as wave flute, you can piece it together by gluing the boards onto a single backing piece. Your backing can be as ordinary as a grocery bag or as elaborate as vellum.

3. This is the design phase. Cut, stamp, punch, decoupage, or other-wise decorate your wraps. (The instructions for the three lamp designs you see here will get you started.) If you're gluing on dimen-sional appliqués, cut and position them, but don't apply them until the assembly stage, after the wrap is secured around the oval frame.

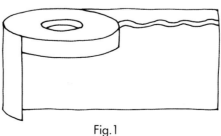

Fig.1

Prep Tip:

If your wrap material is thicker or stiffer than wave-flute or single-face cardboard, add ¼ to ½ inch to the 13⅛-inch length. Wrap it around the edge of an oval temporarily to test the length (see Assembly step 1), and trim it, if necessary. Use the revised length to cut all your remaining wraps.

Design Option:

If you want to cover the tops of your lanterns, transfer the oval pattern to a piece of your wrap material (or another decorative paper), cut out the doughnut shapes, and glue them in place on the lantern tops.

ASSEMBLY

1. Run a thick, solid line of glue along the top long edge of one of your wraps. The line should be as thick as the edge of your cardboard ovals. Place the edge of one of the ovals in the center of the line of glue (see figure 1). Pull up the ends of the wrap around the oval frame, until they meet. While the glue is setting, make sure the top edge of the wrap is even with the top edge of the frame or cover. Let the glue set. Repeat this process to wrap all your ovals.

2. Attach any appliqués you want to add at this point.

3. Insert bulbs in your light cov-ers. Push the bulbs through the tops of the covers (coming in through the center oval). The bulbs' butterfly clips lock into the layers of cardboard. The bulbs should dangle and not touch the sides of the wraps.

Assembly Tips:

• If you've decided to add a decorative edge to your wraps, you may find it's a bit more difficult to glue the wraps evenly to the ovals. Pencil a rule on the inside of the wraps, and use them as your gluing guide.

• If your wraps are wider than 4 inches, they may flare at their bottom edges, making it difficult to glue the ends of the wraps together. Glue a strip of kraft paper or of matching paper stock to the inside of the wraps to solve the problem.

Now that you have the basic steps for assembling your lanterns, here are three options for wraps:

BULBS IN BLOOM

PREP

1. If you're making your own Ovalette, layer your three ovals together.

2. Transfer the pattern on page 121 to the white cardboard and cut out the fence.

3. Punch out the following shapes: three small white flowers, three

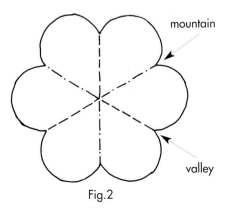

Fig.2

medium purple flowers, two large yellow flowers, and five green leaves.

4. Cut green strands to weave through the posts. Fold the flowers, using figure 2 as a guide.

5. Roughen the fence piece with sandpaper to age it and imitate a wood-grain look.

ASSEMBLY

1. Glue on the fence as your wrap, matching the top line of the fence's cross posts to the edge of the oval frame.

2. Glue on the flowers and the greenery. You can use the project photo as a gluing guide or plant your blooms any way you wish.

LUCKY HEADLINES

PREP

1. If you're making your own Ovalette, layer your three ovals together.

2. From the black wave flute, cut out a wrap strip measuring 1¼ x 13⅛ inches.

3. Cut out five newspaper panels, each measuring 2⅜ x 4 inches.

4. From the red wave flute, cut out an oval cover for your lantern top, if you wish (see Design Option, page 60).

5. On the back side of the wrap strip, mark alternating increments of 2⅜ inches followed by ⅛ inch. Within the 2⅜-inch sections, mark the center.

BULBS IN BLOOM

MATERIALS (FOR ONE LANTERN)

Fence pattern, page 121

Ovalette or 3 C-flute ovals cut from the pattern on page 121

Piece of E-flute white-over-kraft cardboard, 13¼ x 5 inches

4 sheets of wave-flute cardboard, 8½ x 11 inches, in green, purple, white, and yellow

Sandpaper

TOOLS

Cutting mat

Craft knife

Flower hole punches in small, medium, and large

Leaf hole punch

LUCKY HEADLINES

MATERIALS (FOR ONE LANTERN)

Ovalette or 3 C-flute ovals cut from the pattern on page 121

Piece of black wave-flute cardboard, 1³⅛ x 1¼ inches

Sheet of red wave-flute cardboard, 8½ x 11 inches

Chinese newspaper (Check the newspaper section of a well-stocked bookstore.)

Craft glue

TOOLS

Cutting mat

Craft knife

Ruler

Hole punch featuring a Chinese symbol

TIN PUNCH PARTY

MATERIALS (FOR ONE LANTERN)

Ovalette or 3 C-flute ovals cut from the pattern on page 121

Sheet of silver E-flute single-face cardboard, 28 x 36 inches

Craft cement

TOOLS

Cutting mat

Craft knife

Ruler

Decorative-edge scissors

⅛-inch circle hole punch

Teardrop hole punch

Bone folder

Notebook ruler with binding holes

62

Metric Equivalents

⅛"	3 m
¼"	6 m
½"	1.3 c
1"	2.5 c
1¼"	3.1 c
2⅜"	6 c
3⅜"	8.6 c
4"	10.2 c
5"	12.7 c
7"	17.8 c
8½"	21.6 c
11"	27.9 c
13⅛"	33.3 c
13¼"	33.6 c
13½"	34
28"	71.2 c
36"	91.4

6. Slide the hole punch into its maximum depth over the center points you marked in step 5. Punch, and remove the punch pieces, and replace them with punch-outs you make from the red wave flute. It's best to punch and replace one punch at a time, or you risk getting punchy yourself!

7. Center and glue the newspaper pieces onto the back of the wrap strip, on the 2⅜-inch panels.

ASSEMBLY

1. Glue on the cover for your lantern top, if you're adding one.

2. Glue on the assembled wrap strip.

TIN PUNCH PARTY

PREP

1. If you're making your own Ovalette, layer your three ovals together.

2. From the silver single-face cardboard, cut a wrap measuring 13⅛ x 4 inches and a piece of appliqué trim measuring 13½ x 1 inch. Recut the edges of the trim with decorative-edge scissors.

3. All along the wrap, punch out circle and teardrop holes and emboss lines with the bone folder, following the design in figure 3. I left the teardrops on the lanterns shown here half punched for an imitation metal-punch look.

4. To make faux studs on the trim strip, place the strip over the notebook ruler's binding holes, fluted side down. Press the cardboard into the holes with the end of a pen. Ta-da: fake studs!

ASSEMBLY

1. Cement the wrap in place.

2. Cement the decorative trim strip to the wrap.

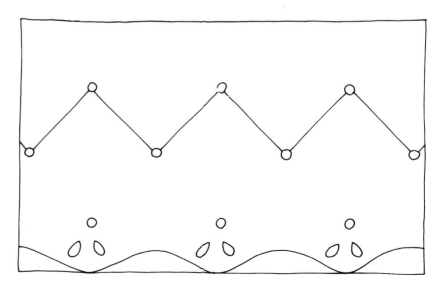

Fig.3

DIVING BOARD

■ Our basic lantern patterns open the door for a dalliance with everyday decor. The Bulbs in Bloom fence posts, for example, would also look adorable with sheep and Bo Peep or Mother Goose and friends. Surround a baby shower buffet table with them, then change to bulbs in soft colors and hang the lanterns in the baby's room. Lanterns with rabbit and egg embellishments would be a perfect choice for a spring dinner.

■ The Asian lanterns become nature's windows when you substitute cardboard strips with vellum backing for the newspaper strips. Choose sheets of leaf-print vellum, and appliqué them with dragonflies. Then, create vertical strips of cardboard with three or so cutout squares in each, so the pieces resemble film strips. Fill the open frames with the vellum. Check your Feng Shui notes to find the right place for lights and luck.

■ Wraps that feature the work of hole punches and decorative-edge scissors make any lantern even more delightful. Plan a pattern of your own, punch it out, then inlay a pretty paper behind it.

CHAPTER FOUR

THE PLUNGE

ON THE COUNT OF THREE, LET'S PLUNGE INTO NEW WATERS. CREATING WITH CARDBOARD MEANS TAKING IT OUT OF ITS USUAL REALM AND TURNING IT INTO SOMETHING THAT MAKES PEOPLE BLURT OUT, "THAT'S CARDBOARD?" THAT'S EXACTLY WHAT THIS CHAPTER IS ABOUT. TOO MANY TIMES, A MATERIAL LIKE CARDBOARD IS CAST ASIDE BY THOSE WHO CAN'T SEE BEYOND ITS TRADITIONAL USES. NOT HERE! WE OFFER A SEA OF POSSIBILITIES FOR WHAT IT CAN BECOME. READ ON, AND IT WON'T BE LONG BEFORE YOU'RE FOLDING, TWISTING, AND EXPLORING THE DEPTHS OF CREATING WITH CARDBOARD. READY?

Call
of the Wild

Shhh! We're hunting a craft of a different culture—the culture of *why not?* Why not rip, tear, and be haphazard? Why not use a stapler to sew cardboard together? There's no way to get lost on this adventure; you're simply exploring new techniques and giving them a try (and likely coming up with some great ideas in the process). When you're finished, you'll be sporting your adventurous spirit with a very vogue mobile phone case. So grab your expedition gear and get going (pith helmet optional).

PREP

1. Enlarge the pattern for the case's main body, and transfer one copy to the back of the black wave-flute board. Enlarge the pattern for the case's sides, and transfer two copies to the back of the black wave-flute board. In addition, transfer two sets of each (two copies of the main body and four copies of the sides) to the grocery bag or kraft paper.

2. Cut out all the pieces and score all the folds on the pieces cut out of black wave flute.

3. Enlarge the animal-print patterns and transfer them to tracing paper. You could also create your own freehand design on tracing paper, using the pattern as a guide. Make a notation on the tracing paper to tell you which side is up (it's easy to accidentally flop this pattern).

4. Flip your traced pattern over. Transfer the small spots marked with a #2 onto the back of the ochre E flute. Transfer the full spot pattern (including the portion marked #2) onto the back of the black wave-flute pieces you cut in step 1. Save your pattern.

5. On all the spots you transferred to the black wave-flute pieces, use the tip of one of your detail scissors to poke a small hole in the center of the #2 portions. Cut out those portions. Also, cut out all the #2 portions on the ochre sheet.

6. Cover one side of each of the pieces you cut out of the grocery bag or kraft paper with glue. Adhere those pieces to the back of the black wave-flute piece. While the glue is still exposed in the openings you cut in step 5, fill each with the corresponding ochre spot.

7. Crush all of your black wave-flute pieces and rescore all the folds.

8. While your wrap and sides are drying, create three strips, which will hide your finished case's stapled seams. First, seam the black single-face cardboard to create an 18-inch strip that's about 1 inch wide, then trim it into three ³⁄₁₆-inch wide strips. If you want to use decorative-edge scissors to trim your strips, make your starting strip 4 inches wide rather than 1 inch wide.

9. Place the tracing paper animal-print pattern (right side up) over the glued pattern pieces, and mark any adjustments on the tracing paper, so it mirrors exactly your glued arrangement on the phone case pieces.

10. With the tracing paper still right side up, transfer the adjusted leopard pattern onto the remaining set of grocery bag or kraft pieces. These pieces become your positioning and tearing guides. Snip a small starting hole into each transferred shape, to start the tears (see photo 1).

MATERIALS

Call of the Wild patterns, page 125 & 126

Piece of black wave-flute cardboard, 3⅝ x 16⅝ inches

Sheets of single-face E-flute cardboard in ochre and black, 8 x 10 inches

Heavy-duty grocery bag or kraft paper with no printing on it

Tracing paper

Craft glue

Closure (I suggest a pronged closure for paper.)

Decorative button (optional)

TOOLS

Cutting mat

Craft knife and sharp blades

Metal ruler or T-square

Bone folder

Small, curved detail scissors

Scraper

Stapler

SUGGESTED REREADING

Transfers to Success, page 16

Scoring, page 19

Seams Like a Winner, page 22

Crushing, page 24

67

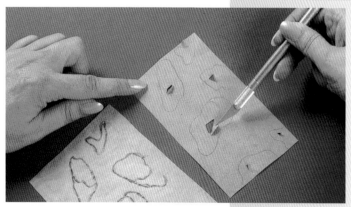

PHOTO 1

Prep Sanity Saver:

When you transfer your animal-print pattern to tracing paper, give each #2 portion its own code (perhaps letter them A, B, C, and so on). Transfer the code to the ochre pieces you cut from the pattern. Then, when it comes time to fit the ochre pieces in place in the black spots (Prep step 6), you'll know which one goes where.

ASSEMBLY

1. Now we're ready for the real therapy part of the process: the tearing, the dismantling of stress, the...actually, it's just plain fun! Apply glue to the unmarked side of the paper bag or kraft paper body piece onto which you transferred the animal-print pattern. Align the piece with the black patterned body piece, and press down. Start the tearing!

Gently guide the tearing with your fingers, to tear out all the spots from the top paper piece, leaving a grocery-bag or kraft-paper top layer with torn-out openings (see photo 2). Wipe away any large deposits of glue. Repeat the process on the case's side pieces.

2. With the bone folder, rescore all the fold lines on the finished pieces.

3. Glue down the two A tabs on the main wrap (refer back to your pattern, if necessary). Hold them securely until they set, then glue down flap B, creating a clean edge for what turns out to be the front lip of the case.

4. Figure 1 shows how to assemble your case. Position the top edge of one side panel to the top edge of the wrap (where flap B is), and align the scores. Staple along the scores. To staple the side panel to the back of the wrap, match the top edge of the side panel to the bottom pair of double-score lines on the back. Then, flip the board over before stapling, so you keep the solid side of the staple on the outside of the seam. When you finish, trim close to the stapled edge, leaving a ¼-inch allowance. Repeat the process to attach the other side panel.

5. Don't despair if your stapled edges aren't as neat as you'd like. The trim strips you prepped earlier become the equivalent of braided trim and camouflage the staples. Apply them by dipping your finger in glue, running the glue along the back of the strips, covering the seams, and trimming off the ends of the trim.

6. Put your phone in your case, and mark where your antenna pops out. Cut a hole in that spot on the case's flap.

7. Attach your closure, following the manufacturer's instructions. Add a decorative button, if you like.

Design Tip:

If you want to hang your case on a clip, attach a grommet at the top of one of the case's back corners.

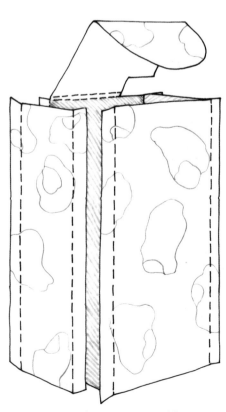

Fig.1 Phone case assembly

PHOTO 2

68

DIVING BOARD

Exposed to the unbridled joy of tearing, you're ready to head in more daring directions—and try some spots of a different color.

■ If you want to make an evening bag instead of a phone case, all you have to do is widen the main body pattern. Keep the same heights and widths of the phone case pattern sides.

■ Domesticate your bag—and give it some glamour. Instead of ochre spots, use gold beads and rods to fill the cutouts. Before you do the tearing technique, cover the beads with a dimensional coating. Instead of kraft paper on top, go with a purple mulberry sheet of paper. Punch holes to add a shoulder strap, if you like. And for a real ensemble, make a wallet to match (see page 39).

■ What else can you use to fill the ochre spots? Try spotted, textured, or striped papers. Mix papers and textures, or maybe switch animals and tear out tiger or zebra stripes instead of leopard spots.

■ Tear your case's top layer to reveal a photo montage or special sayings decoupaged to the case's main body. Cover your photos or sayings with a removable blocker first, so the tear-off layer won't stick.

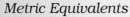

■ Make a paper version of a mola, the vibrant cloth panels made by the Kuna Indians of Panama. Change the color of your case's wave-board layer to green. Cover it with blue single face and tear away a pattern, then layer on yellow and tear away another. Take a look at the appliqué panels of traditional mola designs for inspiration. As a shortcut, use multilayered stencils to create your patterns.

Metric Equivalents

¼″	6 m
³⁄₁₆″	4.8 m
3⅝″	9.2 c
1″	2.5 c
4″	10.2 c
8″	20.3 c
10″	25.4 c
16⅜″	41.6 c
18″	45.7

Cardboard
Bouquet

This set of projects is pure heaven for those who aren't botanically blessed—brown thumbs are definitely welcome. In fact, your thumbs, whatever their color, will play a prominent role as you press the petals of these cardboard flowers and leaves into shape. I've provided instructions for six different types of flowers and foliage. Make them all, then combine them for a fabulous faux display.

ROSIE BEDOSIE

Real roses are named after botanical geniuses, impassioned gardeners, and royalty. Why would ours be any different? My own petite princess, Jessica Rose, lent us her nickname for this first flower project, molded from red and pink cardboard hearts.

PREP

1. Transfer patterns for one center bloom and two small, four medium, and five large petals to the red or pink cardboard, and cut them out.

2. Transfer one leaf bud and two leaf patterns to the green cardboard, and cut them out, using decorative-edge scissors.

3. If you like, decoupage one side of each flower petal with thin, patterned paper. Let the petals dry, then trim the paper. (On the flowers shown here, the decoupaged sides became the bottoms of the petals.)

4. Work all the petals and leaves with your fingers to remove their stiffness. Shape the petals into valleys, with the wave flute falling into them. Roll the tops of the hearts back.

5. Work those thumbs on the fluted side of the leaves to loosen the cardboard. (The fluted sides will become the tops of the leaves.) Dip a finger into the craft glue and apply it to the tops and bottoms of both the split stems of one of the leaves. Overlap one stem over the other, creating an arch down the center of the leaf. Twist and hold the two half stems until they stay together, forming a single stem (see figure 1).

Repeat the process with the other leaf.

6. Roll the rose's center bloom into shape, beginning your roll with side

Fig. 1

A (refer back to your pattern, if necessary). When you're finished, the other edge should overlap side A, and your bloom should resemble the center blooms in the photo.

ASSEMBLY

1. Unroll the center bloom. Along the inside of side A of the bloom, run a line of craft cement. Place ¾ inch of the wire stem into place on the line of cement, and hold it until the cement sets. Reroll the bloom, add a drop of cement to the outside of side A, and press down where it adheres to the other side of the bloom.

2. Curl the tops (the wave side) of the small petals outward. Dab cement on the wave side of their "tails" (the small tabs at the base of the hearts). Cement one right next to the end of the center bloom. Cement the other next to the edge of the first one. You want to add all your petals in one direction—either clockwise or counterclockwise—from the center bloom outward.

ROSIE BEDOSIE

MATERIALS
(FOR ONE ROSE)

Rosie Bedosie patterns, page 122

Sheet of pink or red wave-flute cardboard, 8½ x 11 inches

Sheet of forest green E-flute single-face cardboard, 8½ x 11 inches

Sheet of coordinating paper, 8½ x 11 inches, 20 to 50-pound stock (optional)

18-inch stem of wire wrapped with kraft or green paper (sold in the floral section of craft stores)

Decoupage glue (optional)

Craft glue

Craft cement

TOOLS

Scissors

Decorative-edge scissors

Artist's brush (optional)

SUGGESTED REREADING

Transfers to Success, page 16

BABY BEDOSIE BUD

MATERIALS

Baby Bedosie patterns, page 122

Sheet of red or pink wave-flute cardboard, 8½ x 11 inches

Sheet of forest green E-flute single-face cardboard, 8½ x 11 inches

18-inch stem of wire wrapped with kraft or green paper (sold in the floral section of craft stores)

Craft cement

TOOLS

Scissors

IVY LEAGUE

MATERIALS

Ivy League patterns, page 123

2 sheets of forest or moss green E-flute single-face cardboard, 8½ x 11 inches

Backing paper for the leaves, such as paper with green stripes or checks

Stems of wire wrapped with green paper (sold in the floral section of craft stores) in 10 and 24-inch lengths

Craft glue

TOOLS

Cutting mat

Right triangle

Ruler

Craft knife

Scissors

Round-nose pliers

Sandpaper

SUGGESTED REREADING

Transfers to Success, page 16

3. Crush and roll down the tops of the medium petals, and repress their valleys. Attach two or three of them to the flower, just as you did the smaller petals, and continuing to work in one direction. Your petals can fall close together or they can meet at their edges, depending on how open you want your bloom.

4. Move onto the larger petals, crushing and attaching several in the same way. You can switch back and forth between sizes, according to the look you want. All of your flowers will bloom differently, depending on how you crush and place the petals.

5. Manipulate the leaf bud piece until the three main points (which form the top) pooch out and the six tips curl outward. Dab cement at the center slits of the base and close them. Smudge cement on the inside bottom of the bud leaves and just below the top curls of the leaf tips, then secure the flower base in the leaf bud. When you cement the flower in place, overlap the end leaves of the leaf bud to enclose the flower's bloom.

6. Add two leaves to the wire stem by dabbing cement onto the stem of the leaves and wrapping them around the wire stem. Aah. Stop and take in the beauty of your rose!

Assembly Tip:

Don't wait to form all the petals at the end of assembly; crush and shape as you go. Forming assembled inner petals is difficult, and you risk accidentally "plucking" one out. If you do, it's next to impossible to reinsert a petal.

Follow Your Bloom:

The reason you cut more petals than you may actually use is because each flower blooms in its own way. There's nothing worse than breaking your assembly tempo by stopping to cut more petals. Some flowers may need more small and no large petals. Others may require the reverse. The flower will actually open up and let you know where the petals will go. Feel free to add more leaves, too. You can also make a stem of only leaves for filler if you're creating a bouquet.

Design Tip:

If you wish to add a few friendly thorns to your rose, cut a slice into the paper of the wire stem, being careful not to cut into or through the wire. Pull out the paper wedge created by the slice. With cement on your thumb and finger, roll the wedge to form the thorn (see figure 2).

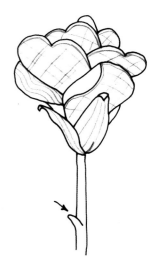

Fig.2

72

BABY BEDOSIE BUD

This sweet little blossom can accompany the large bloom or play quietly amid any bouquet.

Prep and Assembly

1. Transfer the patterns and cut one center bud out of red or pink and one leaf bud out of green.

2. Roll and crush the center bud, creating a "bulging" bud (see figure 3). Start with side A (refer back to your pattern piece, if necessary) when you begin rolling. The wave side can be out or in, depending on the look you want.

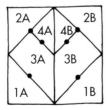
Fig.3

3. Cement the stem in place on edge A. Make sure the stem is glued down ¾ inch up from the bottom of the bud edge, so you won't be able to see it through the top of the bud.

4. Smush and manipulate the leaf bud. It too should have a "bulgy" base look. Simultaneously cement and wrap the leaf bud around the center rose bud.

5. Cut leaves, and add them if you wish.

Design Tip:

Cut into the valley points of the center flower bud to pull the petals back farther if you want a more open bud.

IVY LEAGUE

There are two schools of thought on making great cardboard ivy. The "Board Botanists," who are purists, believe in cutting the leaves out of cardboard with nice, straight cuts. The "Faux Leaf Experts" (FLEs) advocate cutting the leaves out at a 45° angle, then piecing them together so the angles are mirrored, imitating a vein pattern radiating out from the center of the leaf. Don't climb the walls on this one; you can make your ivy either way.

PREP

The Board Botanists simply transfer their patterns to green cardboard and cut. The FLEs follow the system below.

1. Cut one of the sheets of green single-face cardboard into an 8½-inch square.

2. Use the diagram in figure 4 to transfer cutting lines and codes (1A, 1B, and so on) to your square, then cut out all the pieces.

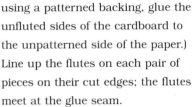

Fig. 4

3. When you nest together opposite pairs of pieces (1A and 1B, for example) on their cut edges, the flutes mimic a leaf's vein pattern radiating out from a spine. Glue the pairs of pieces down on your backing paper, fluted side up. (If you're

using a patterned backing, glue the unfluted sides of the cardboard to the unpatterned side of the paper.) Line up the flutes on each pair of pieces on their cut edges; the flutes meet at the glue seam.

4. Once the glue is dry, you're ready to cut your ivy leaves out of the glued pairs. Transfer the leaf patterns to the glued pairs, using figure 5, page 74, as a guide. The line down the middle of the leaves on the pattern goes on the glued seam. You end up with three leaves of each size.

5. Strip off the twisted paper from the 10-inch wire stems in nine ¾-inch strips. On each ¾-inch strip, unwind one end of the twisted paper and snip out triangle wedges (see figure 6, page 74). The wedges (which look like starlike fingers) will attach to the back center of the leaf and eventually to the main ivy stem.

Prep Tips:

• The cutting diagram in figure 4 can be used on any size square. If

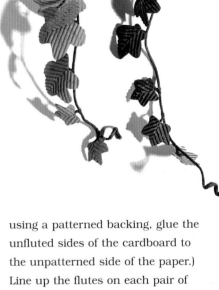

1 medium
1 large

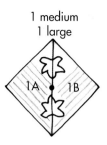

1A • 1B

1 medium
1 large

2A • 2B

2 small

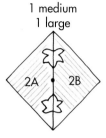

4A   4B

small, medium,
and large

3A • 3B

Fig.5

Fig.6

74

you're cutting from scraps, lay down your scrap cardboard and square it up with the flutes running vertically. Use your right triangle to mark a line at a 45° angle from the far right-hand corner. Flip over the triangle and draw an opposite angle line from a point on the far left-hand side. Cut on the two lines. Glue the two resulting triangles down on backing paper, matching the cut lines to form the central spine for the leaves you'll cut.

• If you want your finished leaves to be more malleable, leave a gap between their spines for embedding wire when you glue them down in Prep step 2. After you cut out the leaf shapes, glue the wire in place. Leave a length of wire at the base of each leaf to wrap around the stem. You can also strip the wire and leave the paper twist to attach to the stem as in assembly steps 2 and 3 below.

ASSEMBLY

There aren't hard-and-fast rules about how you space your ivy leaves on their wire vine or how you shape them once they're there. If you plan to use your vines as filler in a flower arrangement, you may want them less full of leaves. If you're creating stand-alone vines, maybe you want them more lush. Feel free to come up with a combination that suits your situation and style.

1. With your round-nose pliers, make a loose curl at the end of the 24-inch paper-wrapped stem.

2. Dab glue on the bottom of the wedged leaf backs you made in Prep step 5, and stick one onto the back of the base of each leaf. The wedged

fingers should spread out to secure the leaf, and a stem of twisted paper should extend from behind the center of the leaf (see figure 7).

3. An inch or so above the curl you made in step 1, add your first small leaf. Unfurl the stem of the ivy leaf just enough to wrap it around the 24-inch piece of wire (the vine), and hold the leaf in place (again, see figure 7). Dab glue onto the stem, and attach it. Be sure to glue the stem to the underside of the vine; this positions your leaf so it can bob.

4. Plant the next leaf the same way, then continue to sprout

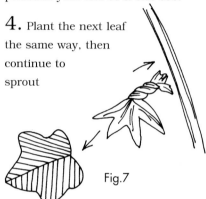

Fig.7

leaves to complete your vine. Spread the distance between the leaves as they get larger.

5. After the glue has set, curl the ends of the leaves with your finger and thumb, giving them more dimension. Run the sandpaper down the center seam of the leaf and out to the other leaf points. The sandpaper highlights provide a finishing touch.

Design Tip:

For a variation, you can make Y-shaped vines. Strip the paper off a second wire, and wrap the clean wire around the main vine until it's secure. Unwind the stripped-off paper twist, then wrap and glue it back over the exposed wire.

FUZZY HOT DOGS

As a child, I always questioned what seemed to me to be obvious absurdities: *How do you look up a word you can't spell? How cute is a bug's ear?* and, the most obvious, *Why call something a "cattail" when it looks exactly like a fuzzy hot dog on a stick?* Now that I'm grown up, I've named our cardboard cattails what I think they really ought to be called.

PREP

1. Transfer the hot dog pattern to the E-flute cardboard, cut the piece out, and score the fold lines.

2. Roll the sides of the piece to break the stiffness of the flutes and form a tube shape. When you've got the shape you want, add glue to the side seam (side A on the pattern), and glue the edges together.

3. Cut 4 inches off the wire stem. Keep both pieces.

4. Use the hot dog leaf pattern to transfer two leaves to the grocery bag or kraft paper. Cut them out, then fold the leaves along their cen-

tral spines and curl and shape them. You don't attach these leaves; you simply insert them into your bouquet.

ASSEMBLY

1. On one end of the hot dog tube, dab craft glue in between the four pagoda-shaped tops. Pinch them together to make a dome shape, but leave open the very top of the dome (see figure 8).

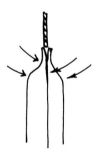

Fig.8

2. Flare back the pagoda tips and coat them with a light layer of craft cement. Run a circle of cement around the 4-inch length of wire stem, 1 inch down from one end. Insert that end into the center of the pagoda tips and pinch the tips together around it.

3. Repeat the process on the other end of the hot dog tube. This time,

MATERIALS

Fuzzy Hot Dog patterns, page 123

Piece of kraft E-flute cardboard, 5⁵⁄₁₆ x 3½ inches

Paper bag or kraft paper

18-inch stem of wire wrapped with kraft paper (sold in the floral section of craft stores)

Craft glue

Craft cement

TOOLS

Cutting mat

Craft knife

Bone folder

Scissors

Sandpaper

SUGGESTED REREADING

Cutting, page 19

MUM'S THE WORD

MATERIALS

Mum's the Word patterns, page 124

Sheet of moss green E-flute single-face cardboard, 8½ x 11 inches

2 sheets of yellow E-flute single-face cardboard, 8½ x 11 inches

Strip of kraft B-flute single-face cardboard, 17⅛ x ⅝ inches

18-inch stem of wire wrapped with kraft paper (sold in the floral section of craft stores)

18-inch stem of wire wrapped with green paper (optional)

Craft cement

Craft glue

TOOLS

Scissors

Decorative-edge scissors (optional)

Round-nose pliers

SUGGESTED REREADING

Transfers to Success, page 16

Rollin', Rollin', Rollin', page 24

though, insert at least 1½ inches of the longer piece of stem wire.

4. Lightly scruff the sandpaper over the entire tube, making the surface fuzzy to the touch. Scruff over the glue seams, too. If necessary, reglue and resand the seams.

5. Clip the wire tip of the hot dog with scissors. The allowance is adjustable, especially if you have several hot dogs in a bouquet. The point height can help differentiate them.

MUM'S THE WORD

You can't keep quiet about a good thing, and the word is out on how easy it is to assemble this beautiful flower. Sure, there are a lot of petals, but the time you invest in making them is well worth the end result. The "secret seed" of this bloom is a Nice Hat Roll (page 25), which provides a perfect little petal pocket that orchestrates the unfolding of the bloom.

PREP

1. Transfer petal patterns to the yellow cardboard, and cut 25 each of the small, medium, and large petals and 35 extra-large petals. This amount probably gives you a few more of each petal than you'll actually use; the exact number you use is up to you. Like the roses, the mum blooms open naturally, and each one will be unique. Trust your eyes, and have confidence in your sense of balance.

2. Crush the petals so they roll slightly at the large ends, fluted side up.

3. Cut a base stem out of the moss green cardboard. You can either transfer the pattern I've provided before you cut, or simply use the pattern as a guide. I made the jagged cuts on both long edges random. If you are inclined, you can certainly break out the decorative-edge scissors for yours.

4. Crush and mold the base stem, working out the middle band to make it bulge. The tips of all the small triangles should flare outward. The body of the large triangles bulge outward, as well, turning the tips inward. You'll curl those tips outward in the final assembly (see figure 9).

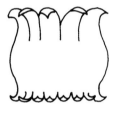

Fig.9

5. Roll the long strip of B flute (our "secret seed") into a small domed Nice Hat Roll (check page 25 for a refresher on this).

6. Wind the green stem (if you've chosen to use one) around the kraft stem. Catch both ends of the stems and make a coil that is the same diameter as the Nice Hat Roll. Push up through the center of the wire coil to make a dome (see figure 10). If you've chosen to use only a kraft stem, make the same coiled dome with your one stem.

Fig.10

Prep Tip:

When cutting the rows of tips on your base stem, it's easier to cut all the angles in one direction first, then reposition your cardboard once and cut all the others.

ASSEMBLY

1. Spread a dollop of craft cement over the top dome of the coiled stem. Insert the dome into the underside of the Nice Hat Roll. Let the cement set. You now have a nice handle (the stem) to hold onto while you insert the petals.

2. Squeeze a blob of craft glue on a scrap of paper; you'll use it for dipping the petal ends. Start by dipping the skinny tip of a small petal and inserting it in the very center of the Nice Hat Roll. Continue to place the petals around and around, following the tiers of the Nice Hat Roll. Work in one direction, with the petals flowing outward. Without crowding, fill the petal pockets as you see fit, gradually increasing the size of the petals. You won't fill every pocket.

3. To complete the bloom, glue a row of extra-large leaves around the outside band of the Nice Hat Roll.

4. Run a thick line of craft glue around the outside row of petals, and wrap the base stem piece, fluted side out, around the base of the bloom. The small-triangle edge runs closest to the petals. The top triangles should flare outward, as if the opening bloom rolled them out. Avoid crushing the wrap around the bloom, so you don't lose the band bulge from the prep phase. When the glue is dry, you can manipulate the leaf tips and seam the raw edge of the wrap.

Metric Equivalents

⅛"	3		5"	12.7 cm
½"	1.3		5⅛"	13 cm
2"	5		5¼"	13.3 cm
3"	7.6		5⅜"	13.7 cm
3⅛"	7.9		5½"	14 cm
3¼"	8.2		5⅝"	14.3 cm
3⅜"	8.6		5¾"	14.6 cm
3½"	8.9		5⅞"	14.9 cm
3⅝"	9.2		6"	15.2 cm
3¾"	9.5		6⅛"	15.5 cm
3⅞"	9.8		6¼"	15.8 cm
4"	10.2		6⅜"	16.2 cm
4⅛"	10.5		6½"	16.5 cm
4¼"	10.8		6⅝"	16.8 cm
4⅜"	11.2		6¾"	17.1 cm
4½"	11.4		6⅞"	17.4 cm
4⅝"	11.8		8½"	21.6 cm
4¾"	12.1		11"	27.9 cm
4⅞"	12.4			

BONUS BLOOM

You can make a baby mum bloom (say that three times fast!) with several adjustments to the full bloom. (Added bonus: The baby bloom doesn't require nearly as many petals.)

1. Prep the wire stem in the same way, and add a Nice Hat Roll on top.

2. Start by inserting a few medium petals, beginning with the third row of flutes in the Nice Hat Roll. Flare the petals the same way you would for the full bloom, but glue them rolling inward, so they imitate a closed blossom. Add a couple of rows of large petals, ending with the extra-large petals to create the shell of the bloom. You don't need to fill every pocket.

3. On the base stem wrap, cut large triangles on both edges. When you apply it, roll the top triangles over the bud, with the tips flaring out, and the bottom triangles in toward the stem, with the very ends of the tips flaring out.

DIVING BOARD

■ Now that you've created a bouquet, stop and smell...wait! Cardboard flowers don't smell. Aah, but they can. Drop some scented oil in the center of all your blooms (somewhere where the oil drop can't be seen), and your flowers will inspire a double take—and a double sniff! Add a different scent to each flower type to create your own floral blend.

■ Snip your blooms, and adorn packages with them in lieu of bows. Use the wrapping paper as the backing on your petals to coordinate the look.

■ Try decoupaging the inside rather than the outside of your flower petals. You could even decoupage them with a photograph—letting the picture develop by overlapping the images on the petals. It would require a few copies of the photo, but what a picture-perfect idea.

■ Have some fun and write a fortune on the back of every petal, then let the recipient pluck a daily good fortune. It's similar to 'loves me, loves me not," with a guaranteed good ending!

■ Try experimenting with drops of bleach or watercolors on the petals and leaves. Imitate dewdrops with a dimensional clear glue. Why not make an entire bouquet in red only, mixing red wave-flute, single-face, and double-embossed cardboard?

Weave
Seen It All

Chances are, you never pictured yourself weaving cardboard, but get ready. Here's a clever project for a mirror frame that allows you to combine a time-honored technique with a new material. The result is striking and, best of all, the process is simple. Over, under, over, under is the rhythmic mantra that becomes so natural you won't even have to think about it. What a relaxing way to create a cardboard project—and one that reflects so nicely on you.

PREP

1. After cutting all the pieces listed on the What to Cut chart, cut a 12-inch square from the center of one of the 18-inch squares.

2. Place the mirror inside the 12-inch opening, and adjust the cardboard frame, if necessary. (You may be surprised to find that the 12-inch measurement of many manufactured mirrors isn't a true 12-inches.) Remove the mirror.

3. If you plan to hang your mirror, use the awl to pierce two even holes in the solid 18-inch square, insert a length of high-gauge wire, and twist the ends of the wire together to make a hanging loop. You need to add your hanger before moving on to the next step.

4. Scrape a layer of glue onto one side of the 18-inch piece with the 12-inch opening. Align it over the solid 18-inch square, and press the pieces together under a stack of books.

5. Squeeze a random pattern of craft cement on the back of the mirror. Place it inside the square frame. Keep those books handy, so you can press this assembly, too. Finally, tape a piece of tracing paper over your mirror to protect it while you weave.

ASSEMBLY

1. Flip your assembled frame over so the solid, 18-inch square faces up. Glue the ends of your various cardboard strips, pattern side up, onto the edges of the solid square, using figure 1, page 82, as your guide for gluing order. Let the glue

MATERIALS

Piece of B-flute cardboard, 36 x 18 inches

3 sheets of kraft single-face E-flute cardboard, 8½ x 11 inches

1 roll of single-face E-flute cardboard in oatmeal

2 sheets of waffle board, 28 x 36 inches, in gray and olive

Several sheets of kraft wave board, 8½ x 11 inches

Mirror, 12 x 12 inches

Short length of high-gauge wire (optional)

Craft glue

Craft cement

Sheet of tracing paper

TOOLS

Cutting mat

Craft knife

Metal ruler or T-square

Triangles

Paper crimper

Awl

Scraper

Heavy books

Toothpick

SUGGESTED REREADING

Be^2, page 17

WHAT TO CUT

Note: When you cut, the flutes of the cardboard should run in the direction of the first dimension provided. For example, on a strip with a measurement of 10 x 1 inches, the flutes should run in the direction of the 10-inch side of the strip.

DESCRIPTION	QTY	MATERIAL	DIMENSIONS
Mirror Base	2	B flute	18 x 18 inches
VERTICAL STRIPS			
Position 1	8	Wave board (kraft)	11 x 9/16 inches
Position 2	6	Single face E flute (oatmeal)	10 x 1 inches
Position 3	4	Waffle board (olive)	18½ x 1⅜ inches
HORIZONTAL STRIPS			
Position 4	6	Waffle board (gray)	22 x 7/16 inches
Position 5	10	Single face E flute (kraft)	8½ x 1⅞ inches

Note: Run these 10 kraft strips through the paper crimper, opposite the flute direction, creating a checkerboard pattern.

Position 6	6	Waffle board (gray)	22 x 7/16 inches
Position 7	11	Single face E flute (oatmeal)	8½ x ¼ inches

on these strips set thoroughly before you move on, or they may pull out while you're weaving. (Remember, if you experience a fit of "Project Fling" with this piece, it could change your luck for the next seven years!)

2. Crush the oatmeal strips completely; they're delicate and might tear otherwise.

3. Turn the assembled frame over, so the mirror side is up. As you weave, you'll bring the strips around the edge of the frame and to the front. Crush each strip at the edge of the mirror frame as you bring it up.

4. As you can see in figure 1, the repeating sections of cardboard

strips fall in 3-inch groupings; the groupings on one edge are marked A in the figure, and the groupings on the other are marked B. Begin by folding over all the B groupings. Then, fold the first A grouping over the edge. Weave each strip in the grouping over and under all the B strips. Continue to fold over the other vertical strips and weave them, beginning each with an opposite weave pattern (for example, if your first strip weaves over, the second strip starts under). As you weave, push each strip down as close as possible to the other strips to achieve a tight weave. Continue weaving across the entire bottom row of squares and then around each side of the mirror.

5. Your strips end at one of two places, either on the back side of the frame or at the edge of the mirror. Finish the ends of the strips that end on the back by folding them over the edge and gluing them down. Some of strips that end at the inside mirror's edge are top strips in the weaving, and others are bottom strips. Finish all the top strips by folding them over the strips directly underneath them and gluing them in place. Finish the bottom strips by gluing them to strips above them. Trim excess.

6. Adhere the weaving to the mirror with a bit of craft cement. Carefully apply the cement with a toothpick to the underside of the finished woven edges framing the mirror. Press and hold until the edge adheres to the glass. Do this one side at a time.

7. Cover the strip ends on the back of the mirror with extra cardboard strips for a nice finish.

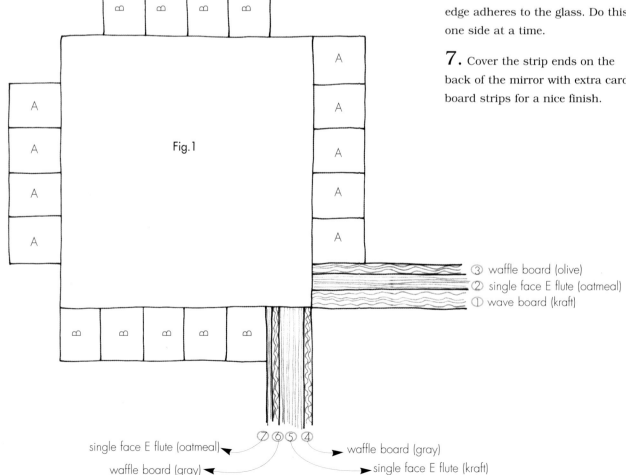

Fig.1

③ waffle board (olive)
② single face E flute (oatmeal)
① wave board (kraft)

single face E flute (oatmeal)
waffle board (gray)
⑦⑥⑤④
waffle board (gray)
single face E flute (kraft)

This weaving pattern is based on repeating 3-inch squares. To create it, the width of each horizontal and vertical repeating grouping of strips adds up to 3 inches. If you want to come up with a different design, you can either change the colors and textures of the strips that make up your 3-inch squares, or you can make your squares larger or smaller.

Assembly Tips:

• Toward the end, you may find your squares aren't weaving evenly. Your corner groupings need to be exact, so go back into your uneven grouping's adjoining 3-inch grouping and trim the vertical strips to realign the uneven weave. I've trimmed some strips myself in the project shown here, and you never would have noticed if I hadn't told you. I give you permission to send your perfection impulse on vacation and trim your strips, too.

• If a strip ends before the end of the row, clip it halfway underneath the closest strip that weaves over it, glue on an extension, and continue weaving.

DIVING BOARD

■ A great source for weave patterns and color schemes is ribbon weaving books. All you need to do is transfer the ribbon widths and color schemes to cardboard strips.

■ Refer back to the Leaving Your Mark section, page 23. Whimsical or thematic impressions are a wonderful way to embellish your strips, and you can position the details so they show up exactly where you want them in your weave.

■ Incorporate different flutes in your weaving pattern, or use hand embossers to create brand-new textures. And don't forget to use plain cardboard; smooth is also a texture.

■ Don't be so neat. Look at cloth weaving for ideas on how to weave with wavy and odd-shaped strips. Or, where we cut and wrapped the ends on this project, don't. Random and uneven ends cut at angles reflect a different woven image.

■ Weaving would also make great material for the E-Zeemoney project, page 39.

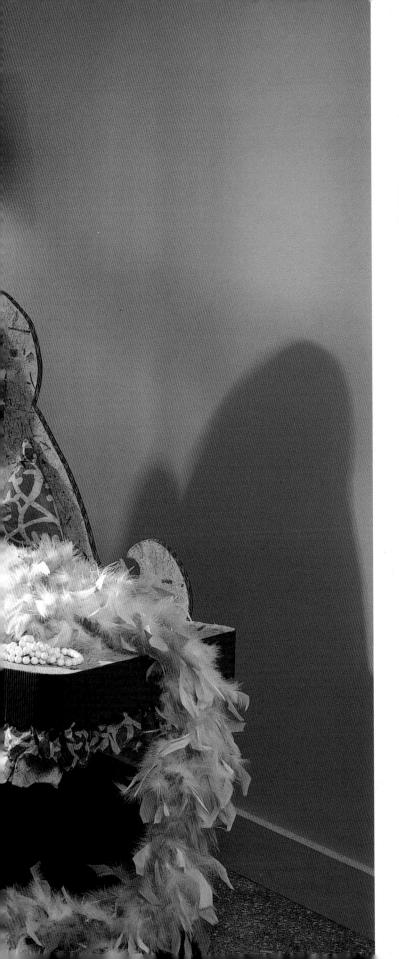

CHAPTER THREE

THE BIG SPLASH

DO YOU REMEMBER THE SUMMERTIME CALL OF
A COOL, SPARKLING POOL? HOT DAYS WHEN
THE SILVER RIPPLES ON THE WATER CAUGHT
YOUR EYE, AND YOU SAW THAT DIVING
BOARD AS YOUR RUNWAY TO RELIEF? RACING
TO THE END OF THE BOARD, CARES FORGOT-
TEN, YOU'RE INTENT ON ONE THING: MAKING
A HUGE SPLASH. THIS CHAPTER IS ABOUT
THAT SPLASH. EACH PROJECT INCLUDES
INSTRUCTIONS FOR CREATING THE FOUNDA-
TION PIECES AND FOR REPLICATING THE
EMBELLISHMENTS YOU SEE IN THE PROJECT
PHOTOS. THERE'S ALSO PLENTY OF ENCOUR-
AGEMENT FOR INTRODUCING YOUR OWN
EMBELLISHMENTS AND CREATING YOUR OWN
ORIGINAL LOOK. SO, CHOOSE A PROJECT,
RACE DOWN THAT DIVING BOARD,
AND…SPLASH!

Mask
of Gazelle-Da

I am fascinated by the vast cultural diversity—yet striking similarities—among masks from around the world. African masks are vibrant and rhythmic in their bold use of color, texture, and shape. Polynesian masks feature an extravagant mix of color, pattern, and symbolism. The mask I've created is a collection of graphic elements that allow your eye to travel over texture, line, and muted colors. It also offers good examples of the "imperfect" symmetry and "casual perfection" that make many masks so exciting. Start with the gazelle canvas I've provided, then use the instructions for replicating this design—or dream up your own.

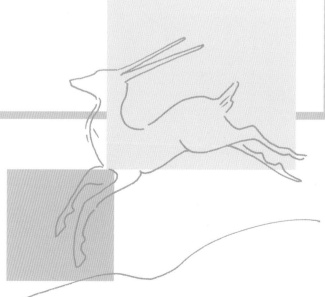

PREP

1. Enlarge the patterns and cut out all the mask base pieces.

2. Score all the folds on the mask, then fold the mask piece into shape, using photo 1 as a guide. Push back on point A at the top of the head while squeezing in on the sides. This drops the forehead back. Score and fold the tabs on their score lines, as well.

ASSEMBLY

1. Glue the horns onto the B tabs on the mask. It doesn't matter whether you glue them to the front or the back.

2. You want to wrap the horns in opposite directions so they become mirror images of each other. Begin with one of the 60-inch horn wrapping strips. Dab glue onto the back end of the strip, and attach it to the front of the horn tab. Wrap and cover the horn tab and horn joint. From this point on, glue down the strip each time you wrap to the back of the horn. Leave the front of the strip unglued, so it creates a raised arc. Wind the strip, dot glue onto the horn where it glues onto the back, and press and hold until it sets. Leave about ³⁄₁₆ inch between each arc near the base. As you wind your way to the top of the horn, the distance between each arc diminishes. Finish by covering the peak of the horn and gluing the strip to the back. Figure 1 shows the horn-wrapping process from the front. When you finish, wrap the other horn, working in the opposite direction.

Fig. 1. Horn wrapping

3. The pair of small braces help hold the shape of the forehead and steady the horns. Fold the braces in half and glue them in place underneath the fold-backs of the forehead and onto the backs of the ears. Refer to photo 2 for exact positioning.

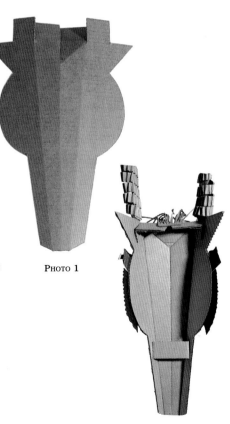

PHOTO 1

PHOTO 2

MATERIALS

CARDBOARD FOR MASK BASE (ALL B FLUTE)

• *Mask: 14 x 19¼ inches*

• *Horns: 1¼ x 13 inches*

• *Braces: 2 pieces measuring 1½ x 2 inches and 1 piece measuring 1½ x 4⅝ inches*

CARDBOARD FOR APPLIQUÉ-TIONS

• *2 strips of C flute single face (for horn-wrapping strips), ¾ x 60 inches*

• *1 sheet of metallic copper single face, 11 x 17 inches*

• *6 sheets of E flute single face, 8½ x 11 inches, 1 black, 1 ochre, 2 white, and 2 burgundy*

• *2 sheets of C flute single face, 8 x 10 inches, 1 black and 1 ochre*

• *1 sheet of black wave flute, 8½ x 11 inches*

• *1 strip of kraft E flute, 2 x 6¾ inches, (for hair)*

OTHER MATERIALS

Mask of Gazelle-Da patterns, page 127-132

Craft glue

Craft cement

TOOLS

Cutting mat

Craft knife

Metal ruler or T-square

Bone folder

Scissors

Decorative-edge scissors, including "mountain" scissors, which cut a large zigzag pattern

Punches: ½-inch circle, ⅜-inch circle, ⅛-inch circle, ¼-inch square, small swirl

Embossers: crimper and diamond pattern

SUGGESTED REREADING

Cutting, page 19

Scoring, page 19

Leaving Your Mark, page 23

4. Cement the larger brace about 5 ⅜ inches up from the bottom of the nose.

Horn Wrapping Alerts & Options

■ The wrapping direction on the back of the horn is opposite from the front, and the spacing on the back may not look the same as it does on the front. Don't worry about this. Pay attention to how the wrapped strips look on the front and not the back.

■ For a solid horn, an extended Nice Hat Roll (page 25) works well. You can even make a multicolored horn by stacking a series of colored rolls. Wrap the first roll right around the horn tab to anchor your solid horn.

APPLIQUÉ-TIONS

My mask design is a series of mirrored and mismatched images I cut by hand and eye, not by precise measurements. If you want to re-create this exact design, trace the patterns or try them freehand. Note the direction of the board marked on the patterns. Some of the punched shapes create elements for more than one set of facial features. The punched-out piece is used on one, for example, and the silhouette it leaves is used on another. Use the project photo as a guide for assembling and gluing the appliqué elements. It's also a great starting point for creating your own mask, whether you want to alter the color scheme, the appliqué shapes, or both.

1. Cut out the appliqués, following the notes on the pattern pieces about the color and type of cardboard you need for each piece. In addition, follow the pattern notes about which pieces need to be embossed or otherwise embellished.

■ For the long strip running down the nose, seam the white single face first, and run it through the diamond embosser. Following the embossing pattern, cut out the edge to create the zigzag border. Punch it down the center with the square and circle hole punches. Lay this finished piece down on the back of the copper single face. Trace an ample outline around the white strip, then cut the copper piece by hand or use decorative-edge "mountain" scissors.

■ For the main eye pieces, in addition to cutting out the two pieces for your mask, cut an extra, then cut the extra piece apart at the score lines. You can use these cut pieces as scoring guides, because you'll need to make scores on both sides of the main eye pieces (and you won't want drawn score lines on the front). With your bone folder, follow the pattern markings and use your guides to trace the eye piece's smallest circle from the back side. Trace the middle circle from the front side and the largest from the back. (See photos 3 through 5.) Now cut the slit through the middle of the eye. From the front side, start to pinch up the first (smallest) circle by squeezing the score between your thumb and forefinger. Pinch all around the circle. Pinch from the back to make a valley around the center circle line. Pinch the largest

circle from the front side, just as you did the smallest. Where the slit starts at the inner edge of the eye, bring together the two pinched ends and overlap them slightly. They should naturally nest. Glue the overlap together and hold it until the glue sets (see photo 6). Repeat the process with the other eye piece.

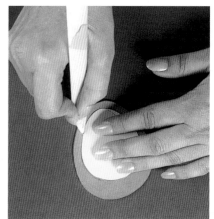
PHOTO 3

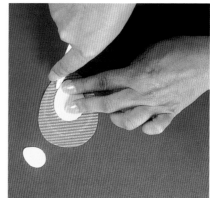
PHOTO 4

PHOTO 5

88

Photo 6

giving some decorative edges and others straight edges. The effect helps to move your eye along the entire piece. You can cut the zigzag ochre strip that runs along the side of the mask by eye, using regular scissors, or with decorative-edge scissors. Try mismatching decorative-edge scissor blade cuts or using two different blades for different patterns.

2. Position all the appliqués on the mask, using the project photo as a guide.

3. You can apply the appliqués one of two ways. You can glue the mulit-layer "sets" together (the four pieces that form the eye, for example), position all the glued sets, then glue the sets in place. Or, you can glue down the layers of each set one at a time.

4. On the 2 x 6¾-inch hair piece, cut ⅛-inch strips parallel to the long edges. Leave about ½ inch on one short end. Glue the solid short end to the top of the mask's recessed forehead.

Appliqué-tion Tips:

■ Note where the folds on the mask are. If you're creating your own appliqués rather than using the patterns provided, you need to add more cardboard to any piece that wraps over folds.

■ Use decorative-edge scissors alternating with hand cuts on the pieces,

Metric Equivalents

⅛"	3 mm
3/16"	5 mm
¼"	6 mm
⅜"	9.5 mm
½"	1.3 cm
¾"	1.9 cm
1¼"	3.1 cm
1½"	3.8 cm
2"	5.1 cm
4⅝"	11.7 cm
5⅜"	13.7 cm
6¾"	17.1 cm
8"	20.3 cm
8½"	21.6 cm
10"	25.4 cm
11"	27.9 cm
13"	33 cm
14"	35.6 cm
17"	43.2 cm
19¼"	48.9 cm
60"	152.4 cm

DIVING BOARD

■ You've gathered enough techniques from the earlier chapters to design masks of your own—celestial masks, goddess masks—the possibilities are endless. Go to a bookstore or library and look at masks from all over the world. Create a flat mask and layer color, or build up layers with Rolli-Os or Floutist Rolls (see page 25) as support features and decorative accents. Roll, shape, tear—each of these methods will bring your theme to life.

■ Find a face that launched a thousand ships. Look at sculptures and paintings from the past for inspiration. Cameos provide some excellent profiles to imitate.

■ Change your point of view and research Pablo Picasso, Georges Braque, or Marcel Duchamp. Looking at art from the cubist period will help you break down facial features into basic art elements.

■ You don't need to travel around the world or through time to find a face. Look in your family photos or grab your camera and snap shots of a few of your favorite faces, then create masks based on what you see. Your 3-D family gallery will definitely be one of a kind.

United We Stand
Divider

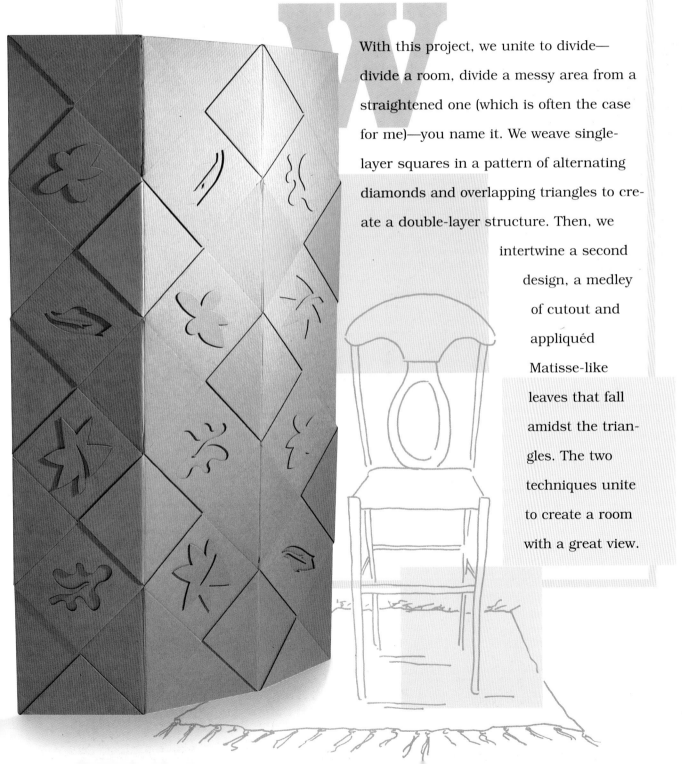

With this project, we unite to divide—divide a room, divide a messy area from a straightened one (which is often the case for me)—you name it. We weave single-layer squares in a pattern of alternating diamonds and overlapping triangles to create a double-layer structure. Then, we intertwine a second design, a medley of cutout and appliquéd Matisse-like leaves that fall amidst the triangles. The two techniques unite to create a room with a great view.

Metric Equivalents

¼" 6 mm

18" 45.7 cm

PREP

1. Mark the centers on all four sides of each square. From each center point, mark spots ¼ inch to the right and left. Join the center points and the exterior points of each adjoining side with pencil lines (see figure 1). These lines will become either score or glue lines.

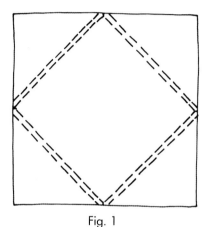

Fig. 1

2. Following the folding patterns in figure 2, score and fold the squares: two each of folding patterns A, B, and C; six of folding pattern D; and three of folding pattern E.

3. Lay out the squares, following the assembly diagram in figure 3. Lightly pencil a number on each square, starting with 1 at the bottom left square, up to square 5. Square 6 will be the bottom middle square, and the other squares in that column will go up to square 10. The last column starts with square 11 and goes up to square 15. (The penciled-in numbers help, because you disassemble the piece to embellish the squares, then reassemble it.)

4. Make copies of the patterns on page 133 to use as stencils.

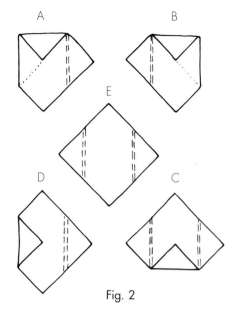

Fig. 2

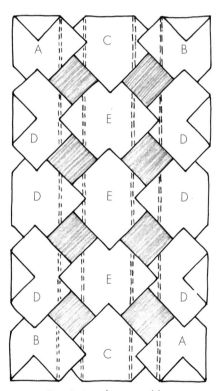

Fig. 3. Divider assembly

5. You can use the patterns to create cutout or raised leaf shapes on some or all of the squares. The cutout you create on one square (if you cut careful, clean lines) becomes the raised shape for another square. (Note that none of the cutouts shows all the way through the finished divider. Because of the weaving technique we use to assemble the squares, every cutout is backed by a piece of cardboard.) The number and placement of cutouts and raised shapes are up to you. Pencil the leaf patterns down where you want them, noting which you want to be cutouts and which you want to be raised leaves.

6. Cut the cutout shapes from each designated square, using your craft knife and a sharp blade. Run the blade around the perimeter of the design, just cutting through the top layer of paper. To finish the cutting, you may find it easier to hold the area being cut off the edge of your worktable. Use your craft knife in a sawing motion around the pre-cut line to remove the shape.

7. If you've been careful, you can glue this cutout onto one of your panels needing a raised shape. Smooth a thin layer of glue onto the back of the shape, and press it onto the panel, using the penciled outline as your guide.

8. Stack the squares in order (top to bottom) in the three columns where they belong, following your penciled numbers.

ASSEMBLY

1. Glue in place all of the folded sections indicated on squares A, B, C, and D.

2. Line up the first column of squares (marked 1-5); you will line up sides, corners, and the double scores. Glue them together where they overlap.

3. Attach the middle column of squares to the first column, one square at a time, starting at the bottom (square 6). Align the double scores in the middle column to those in the first column.

4. Glue on the final column of squares, one at a time, matching folds, scores, and the penciled glue lines you marked in Prep step 1.

5. Once the glue sets, rescore and refold all the double scores. These scores create your divider's "hinges." Rescoring and refolding keep them from locking.

Assembly Tips:

■ When gluing in place a square with a cutout shape, scrape a layer of glue onto the back side of the cut square, and remove any glue that seeps up over the cutout edges. You want no glue on the fronts; it will discolor the cardboard.

■ The points of the squares don't meet exactly in the middle of the squares they're overlapping, and they don't lie right next to each other. You'll notice approximately ¼ inch of spacing difference.

DIVING BOARD

■ This monochromatic divider makes a subtle accent piece in the midst of a busy environment, but you don't have to stop there. Try painting your squares with three different shades of the same color, or add a subtle pattern to your divider with a decorative foam stamp.

■ Black and white checks with giant green pimento olives—why not? It could be the ultimate statement for a divider meant for a playroom. Mix it up with some random pink elephants for a whimsical touch.

■ Decoupage the squares with designer sheets of tissue paper for a classic collage look. Tissue patterns are manufactured in fabulous designs you can mix and match for an interesting duet: solids and patterns, stripes and checks. Push the limits!

■ Need a divider on a smaller scale? Reduce the size of the squares and create a divider to camouflage kitchen clutter or desk overflow. On a smaller divider, you can cut frames into your squares for photo inserts (corrugated paper is typically acid free, but when in doubt, use photocopies instead of actual photos). Use cardboard that's a smaller flute size if you're making a smaller divider—E flute or F flute would both work well.

■ Keep the width of this design, but reduce the number of squares glued on for height, and you've got a divider that's the perfect size for a decorative fireplace screen. (Just be sure to remove it when you've actually got a fire burning!)

■ Play peekaboo. Cut windows all the way through your divider, then dress them. Lacy natural papers or vellum sheets let the light come through while continuing to discreetly mask what's behind the screen. Glue them in between the divider's overlapping panels.

Forest
Trunk

To paraphrase a philosophy recently recited on the silver screen, life is like a box of cardboard: You never know what you're going to get—or what you'll find inside. Use your box to make this ample-sized trunk, and you can fill it with everything from treasures and toys to out-of-season clothing. The patterns for Forest Trunk are surprisingly simple, and assembling the pieces requires nothing more than some basic cutting and folding techniques. Finish with some easy cutting and crushing, and you can cover your trunk with a forest of branching cardboard trees.

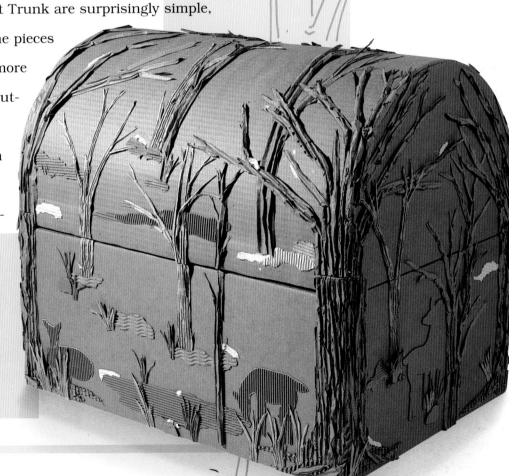

MATERIALS

CARDBOARD FOR TRUNK

• Base: B flute, 49⅛ x 55¼ inches

• Wrap for lid top: C flute single face, 20⅝ x 26¾ inches

• Strips for lid top: 2 pieces of B flute, 19⅝ x 1½ inches each

• Lid ends: 2 pieces of B flute, 18¼ x 14⅝ inches each

CARDBOARD FOR APPLIQUÉ-TIONS

• Single-face strips in all flutes and neutral colors, cut in widths ranging from ⅜ to 4 inches

OTHER MATERIALS

Forest Trunk patterns, pages 134 and 135

Craft glue

Craft cement

Metal hinges (optional)

Paper-wrapped wire for lock (Check the floral sections of craft stores.)

TOOLS

Cutting mat

Craft knife

Metal ruler or T-square

Bone folder

Scissors

SUGGESTED REREADING

Scoring, page 19

Seams Like a Winner, page 22

PREP

1. Transfer the patterns and markings for the base and lid, cut out the pieces, and score all the fold lines.

2. On the C-flute wrap (lid top), mark a ½-inch strip down both long edges. Crush the strip with the side of your bone folder. If you want to decoupage or color the wrap, which becomes your trunk lid, do so now.

3. The fluting on your trunk lid can appear on either the inside or outside. Determine where you want it before moving on to assembly.

ASSEMBLY

1. Center the lid top over the two ends, just to check position (see figure 1). The crushed ½-inch strips on the lid top will fit into the lid ends in Assembly step 2. At the other lid ends, you'll have extra cardboard. Glue the extra cardboard under at each end, to make clean edges, then glue the 19⅝-inch strips to the inside of these folded ends for extra strength.

2. Sandwich the crushed ½-inch strips on the lid top between the arcs of the lid ends. To glue the strips in place, run a 4-inch section of glue on the inside of one lid end, insert a strip, and press it to the glue. Remove any excess glue, and hold the wrap until the glue sets. Glue all of the wrap down in this manner, then run a line of glue on the open side of the lid end, and press it over the other side of the wrap. Repeat this process on the other end of the lid (see figure 2).

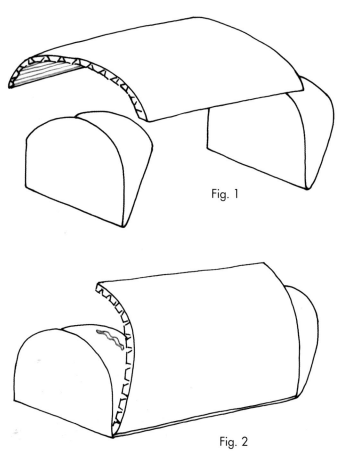

Fig. 1

Fig. 2

3. Using figure 3 as a guide, fold the trunk base into a box shape. First fold in the A flaps, then fold the B panels in over them. The B flaps rest on the side of the box, and the side pieces close in over them, creating three layers from one piece.

4. Skip down to the Appliqué-tion steps and add embellishments now, keeping in mind where you'll later attach your hinges.

5. Attach the hinges to the finished trunk.

APPLIQUÉ-TIONS

THREE-STEP TREES

Use the photographs and general instructions that follow to assemble your own forest of appliqués for your trunk.

1. Cut a strip of single face or wave flute, with the flute direction running vertically. Cut several slits down one, two, or three flutes or more, depending on how thick you want your tree trunks (see photo 1).

2. Spread these slits out while crushing the flutes, creating the first set of branches and starting to texturize the bark (see photo 2). Continue to split the individual branches into smaller and thinner branches. Bring the final branch tips to a point by clipping the tips with scissors (see photo 3).

3. Make a rougher bark by using your craft knife to make slits in the flutes, then fold them open to give them depth. You can add more single face to create an even more dimensional trunk.

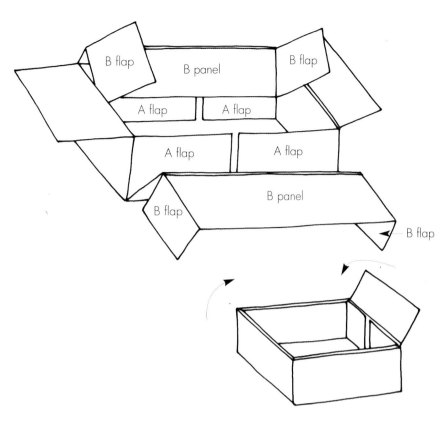

Fig. 3. Forest Trunk assembly

Photo 1

Photo 3

Photo 2

HINGING AND LATCHING TREES

In lieu of actual hinges, you can create cardboard tree hinges on the back of your trunk. Glue a small piece of fabric underneath the unfluted side of the trees that will run over the seam where the lid and trunk meet for a more durable hinge. To make your own trunk latch, embed a length of paper-covered wire approximately 1 inch long inside one of the tree trunks at the center of the lid, and glue it in place with craft cement. Leave the end sticking out, and loop it. When you glue down the tree on the base of the trunk below the loop, make the tree's trunk wide enough and slightly raised, to accommodate the wrapped loop.

ADDING OTHER DESIGN ELEMENTS

If you like, decorate your forest with kraft-colored deer (using the patterns on page 135), blue lakes (use your bone folder to add water rings), and hand-torn patches of snow. The balance of your ecosystem is up to you.

Metric Equivalents

3⁄8"	9.5 mm
1⁄2"	1.3 cm
1"	2.5 cm
1½"	3.8 cm
4"	10.2 cm
14⅝"	37.2 cm
18¼"	46.3 cm
19⅜"	49.8 cm
20⅝"	52.4 cm
26¾"	67.9 cm
49⅛"	124.8 cm
55¼"	140.3 cm

DIVING BOARD

■ Add appliqués of other woodland creatures and features. Cut silhouettes of moose, bears, and other animals, and use textured cardboard for their fur, or use green cardboard and grow some instant pine trees for a more lush-looking forest.

■ Transfer some techniques from the Weave Seen It All project, page 80, and cut your animals or other features out of pieces of woven cardboard. You can weave together a variety of looks, from country plaid to bold Scottish tartan. Trace and cut out your shape from card stock, weave a square large enough to cover your shape, then glue the weaving onto the shape and trim it out.

■ Because single-face cardboard is easy to shape, why not construct a royal chest by turning the arced edges of the lid into the three points of a crown? Add jolly king and queen faces at both ends. "Toys Rule" can be the motto on a coat of arms displayed on the sides.

■ Instead of building a castle, build a home by turning the ends of the lid into triangles that create a peaked roof. Add window curtains and doors for that lived-in look.

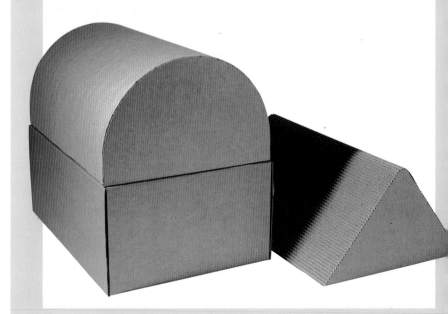

French Groove
Rolltop Desk

O"Oui," being the French word for "yes," should be your enthusiastic response to the idea of making this desk decorated with Provencal-style appliqués. Rolltop desks have fascinated me since childhood, especially their mysterious doors that glide up and out of sight (where do they go?). It's those doors that started me thinking, but the project didn't come into focus until I took a new look at my mother's childhood rolltop desk. I realized single-face cardboard could act like the jointed wood rolltop, and a simple pair of grooves could guide the gate.

MATERIALS

CARDBOARD FOR DESK

- *Box: B flute, 40¹⁵⁄₁₆ x 40¾ inches*

- *Groove side panels: 4 pieces of B flute, 10 x 9⅝ inches each*

- *Back: B flute, 14½ x 9⅝ inches*

- *Roll support: B flute, 14 x 1 inches*

- *Rolltop: B flute single face, 14⁵⁄₁₆ x 14¾ inches*

- *Back seam covers: 2 strips of E flute single face, 2½ x 10 inches each*

CARDBOARD FOR DESK FEET

- *4 strips of red E flute single face, 11 inches, cut so they taper (They should be 1¼ inches wide at their wide ends and ¼ inch wide at their narrow ends.)*

- *4 strips of green E flute single face, ½ x 8¼ inches, cut so they taper (They should be ½ inch wide at their wide ends and ³⁄₁₆ inch wide at their narrow ends.)*

- *4 strips of kraft B flute single face, ¾ x 10½ inches*

CARDBOARD FOR APPLIQUÉ-TIONS

- *Assortment of 5 x 7-inch pieces of single face B flute in ochre, blue, red, green, kraft, and black (These pieces are often sold in packages of assorted colors. You'll need approximately 2 packages, or 4 pieces of each color.)*

- *Piece of cream wave flute, 8½ x 11 inches*

- *Strip of red wave flute, 3½ x 15⅞ inches*

- *Strip of green wave flute, 1 x 9 inches*

OTHER MATERIALS

French Groove patterns, pages 136-139

Craft glue

Wax candle

TOOLS

Cutting mat

Craft knife

Metal ruler or T-square

Hole punches (circles and triangles)

Bone folder

SUGGESTED REREADING

Crushing, page 24

Rollin', Rollin', Rollin', page 24

PREP

1. Using the patterns beginning on page 136, cut the box and groove side panels out of B flute and the appliqués out of the colors of B flute single face specified on the pattern pieces. In addition, cut several dozen ¼-inch and 1-inch squares and punch some small circles and triangles in a variety of colors to use as appliqué accents.

2. Score all folds on the box piece, and fold all the scores.

3. Glue together the groove side panels, aligning the front arcs, so you end up with two double-layer panels.

4. Glue the double-layer groove side panels onto the A panels of the box, matching the front arcs, to create triple-thick panels on each side of the box. You'll be left with a space between the back of panel K of the box and the groove side panels. This space accommodates the rolltop.

5. Center and glue the back panel into place on the outside of panel K of the box. The back panel provides added strength. Let all the glued panels set.

6. Crush ¼ inch strips on each of the 14⁵⁄₁₆-inch edges of the rolltop piece. (The flat side of your bone folder works well for this.) Run the

wax candle over the front and back side of the ¼-inch strip.

7. If you want appliqués on the rolltop piece, glue them on now. When you insert this piece in the desk, you can do so with the fluted side facing out or in. If you plan to have the fluted side face in, glue a flat strip of paper onto the ¼-inch edges of the fluted side, so the piece will roll smoothly. Crush and wax these strips, as well.

8. In the center of one 14¾-inch edge of the rolltop, punch or cut out a handle hole about ¼ inch up from the edge. Using the hole as a guide, punch a matching hole in the roll support, and glue the 14 x 1-inch roll support to the back of the edge for strength.

9. Run a fold score line ½ inch in from the edge of the 10-inch sides of the back seam covers.

Prep Variations:

■ If you want to design your own appliqués rather than use the patterns provided, it's easier to design them on the assembled piece. Create tracing-paper shapes, transfer them to the colored cardboard, and cut them out. After assembling the desk, place the appliqués on the board, tweak the shapes and their placement if necessary, add or remove appliqués, then glue them on.

■ Rather than cutting a hole for a handle in Prep step 8, you could make a knob from a roll. Refer to page 24 for a variety of roll options.

ASSEMBLY

Use figure 1 as a guide when assembling your desk.

1. Fold up the C and E strips. Add glue into the seams of the G panel, where it joins the A panels. Spread glue onto the outside of the C panels.

2. Fold over the D panel, placing the C strips on the glue lines on the seams of the G panel. Fold up the A panels and hold them in place until the glue sets.

3. Begin inserting the rolltop piece from the back of the configuration, beginning with the end with the finger hole or knob (see figure 2). Don't insert the piece all the way. The rolltop should be in its open position when you move onto the next steps.

4. Drizzle glue on top of the B tabs and inside the H and J panels.

5. Fold up panel K. Fold panel J over the B tabs and wrap panel H under the B tabs (see figure 3). This is tricky, so work it slowly, being careful not to dent your sides. You may want to try the assembly without glue first. If you have problems, remove the rolltop piece and work it in after you've glued the other pieces in place.

6. Glue the back seam covers over the back open seams of the construction, aligning the folds with the seams (see figure 4). The ½-inch side of each cover goes to the back.

APPLIQUÉ-TIONS

Use the project photo as a guide when adding your own appliqués.

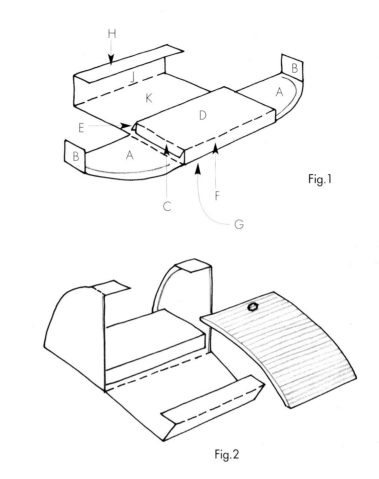

Fig.1

Fig.2

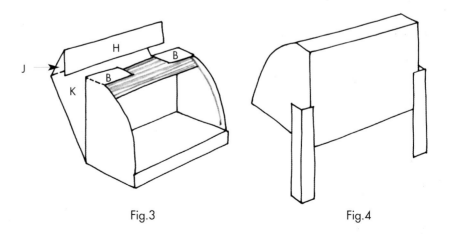

Fig.3

Fig.4

Metric Equivalents

3/16"	5 m
1/4"	6 m
1/2"	1.3 c
3/4"	1.9 c
1"	2.5 c
1 1/4"	3.1 c
2 1/2"	6.4 c
3 1/2"	8.9 c
5"	12.7 c
7"	17.8 c
8 1/4"	20.9 c
8 1/2"	21.6 c
9"	22.9 c
9 5/8"	24.5 c
9 3/4"	24.8 c
10"	25.4 c
10 1/2"	26.7 c
11"	27.9 c
14"	35.6 c
14 5/16"	36.4 c
14 1/2"	36.8 c
14 3/4"	37.5 c
15 7/8"	40.3 c
40 3/4"	103.5 c
40 15/16"	104 c

FRONT LIP

Score the back of your front lip piece, following the score line on the pattern. Glue it in place on the front of your desk base, nesting the notches into the groove side panels. Add 1/4-inch accent squares underneath the piece.

ROLLTOP

1. Glue the knob backing in place on the handle edge of the rolltop piece.

2. Make a Floutist Rolli-O Roll (a Floutist Roll with a large hole in the center) to serve as your desk's knob, with the center of the roll matching the size of the hole you cut in Prep step 8. Glue the knob in place, aligning all the holes. Center a pair of swirls on either side of the handle, and glue them in place. Add teardrop accents above the swirls.

TOP OF DESK

Glue down a series of 1-inch squares, accented with a couple of circle swirls.

DESK SIDES

On the edges of each side, glue down color bars of squares and/or alternating colors of triangles, swirls, or dots, depending on the look you want. On one side, glue down the apple and apple wedge. On the other, glue down the pear and the pear half. Cut two tiny teardrop shapes from a dark color of single face, and glue them on as seeds in the white portion of the pear half.

FEET

Refer back to the Rollin', Rollin', Rollin' instructions, page 24, to create your desk's feet.

1. Roll the red strips into Nice Hat Rolls.

2. Roll the green and kraft strips into Floutist Rolls.

3. Once you have rolls for all four feet, glue the feet together in the following order: red, green, kraft.

4. Mark placement points on the desk's bottom corners and glue on the feet. Whether you inset them slightly from the corners of the box is up to you.

Tip:

When you're rolling the pieces for your desk's feet, roll all the rolls in one color first, then move on to the second and third colors, making sure all the rolls that are the same color are also the same height and width. It's easier to adjust a portion of an unglued roll than it is to add or subtract height or width from a glued one.

DIVING BOARD

■ Ali Baba, so the story goes, stood in the front of a massive stone wall, uttered two magic words—*open sesame*—and the stone wall separated to let him and his entourage into their secret den. But the million-dollar question is: Did the stones slide up like a rolltop desk or open up like French doors? With cardboard, your doors can open any way you want. Try setting this desk on its side—it would fit perfectly into a corner—so the door opens sideways. (You could even stash candy inside, and decoupage the door with its labels.)

■ Change the whole shape of the desk by creating a box with half-cylinder panels for the top and bottom. Make grooves on the panels to allow two doors to peel away from the center. This design creates the perfect console for a music or cosmetics collection.

■ For a different groove, cut a wavy path for the door to follow.

■ Feet made of shiny glass baubles would be a nice accent if you make your desk from metallic cardboard. Or, for a more natural approach, use stacked stones for feet.

Curlicue
Curio Cabinet

The cardboard you need for this colorful cabinet is a standard school supply. You'll find it in parent-teacher stores and craft shops, sold as material for triptych display boards. Though it's not the sturdiest form of cardboard, it works well for a project of this size. Top the standard box with a few festive rolls, add some feet, and you've got a cabinet with definite personality.

PREP

1. Using the patterns on page 140 and 141, cut out all the cabinet pieces, and score all the folds.

2. Temporarily assemble the box, using figures 1 and 2 as guides, and check all measurements. If you need to tweak a piece, now is the time.

A. Place the red back insert panel on the inside center panel of the box body, uncolored sides together.

B. Fold in the side flaps of the box top and bottom pieces (the blue and yellow pieces), and lay them in the folds surrounding the center panel of the box (see figure 1).

C. Fold up the sides of the box body, enclosing the side flaps of the box top and bottom.

D. Fold over the ends of the box top and bottom, enclosing the flaps of the box body (see figure 2).

E. Run the flat side of your bone folder over the ⅜-inch edges on the sides of the box body to make flat, crisp folds around the perimeter of the box.

3. Fold over the door panel and try its fit in the opening of the box body, using the 12-inch dowel as a rod in the fold of the door.

4. If everything fits, unassemble the cabinet. If your pieces don't fit perfectly, adjust them where necessary or recut problem pieces.

5. Fold over the two panels of the door. Crease the center fold with your scoring tool, and reopen it. The inside panel is the slightly smaller one.

6. In this step, you'll cover the raw top and bottom edges of the door. Lay your door flat, front side down, and run slit scores through the two lines marked A on the pattern piece. Be sure not to cut through to the front of the board. From the slit marks, strip the flutes off the board all the way across the top and bottom of the piece; you'll just be stripping a ¼-inch line along each edge (see figure 3, page 106). Run your scoring tool along the stripped edges of cardboard. Fold the stripped paper over to cover the raw edges of the board. If your cuts are even, there should be enough to roll over the edges and onto the other side, which becomes the inside of the door panel. Smear glue on the stripped paper flaps and secure

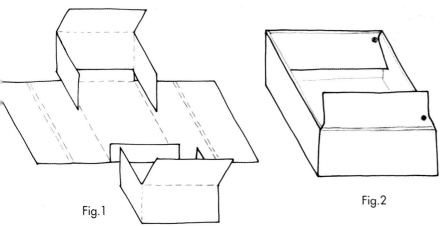

Fig.1

Fig.2

MATERIALS

CARDBOARD FOR CABINET

Use cardboard from colored, three-panel project boards. You'll find the boards at parent-teacher stores or in the school supply section of well-stocked craft stores.

- Box body: green, 28¼ x 16 inches

- Box top: blue, 9⁹/16 x 21½ inches

- Box bottom: yellow, 9⁹/16 x 21½ inches

- Back insert: red, 11½ x 9¼ inches

- Door: red, 18 x 11¾ inches

CARDBOARD FOR APPLIQUÉ-TIONS

- 12 strips of colored B-flute cardboard, 1½ x 24 inches, 4 red, 4 yellow, 2 blue, 2 green

- 1 strip of blue B-flute cardboard, 1½ x 7 inches

- 1 strip of green B-flute cardboard, 1½ x 8 ¾ inches

- 4 sheets of single-face E-flute cardboard, 8½ x 11 inches, in orange, yellow, green, and blue

- 3 sheets of wave-flute cardboard, 8½ x 11 inches, in purple, red, and green

- 2 sheets of vellum, 8½ x 11 inches, 1 with purple polka dots and 1 with purple checks (optional)

- 1 sheet of white card stock, 8½ x 11 inches (optional)

- 1 sheet of permanent double-stick adhesive, 8½ x 11 inches (optional)

OTHER MATERIALS

Curlicue Curio Cabinet patterns, pages 140 & 141

Craft glue

Wooden dowel, 12 inches long, ¼ inch wide

Watercolor pens or acrylic paint in colors that match your cardboard colors

Sealer

Metric Equivalents

⅛"	3 mm
¼"	6 mm
⅜"	9.5 mm
1½"	3.8 cm
3¾"	9.5 cm
4½"	11.4 cm
7"	17.8 cm
8½"	21.6 cm
8¾"	22.2 cm
9³⁄₁₆"	23.3 cm
9¼"	23.5 cm
9⁵⁄₁₆"	23.7 cm
11"	27.9 cm
11½"	29.2 cm
11¾"	29.8 cm
12"	30.5 cm
16"	40.6 cm
18"	45.7 cm
21½"	54.6 cm
24"	61 cm
28¼"	71.8 cm

them over the edges and onto the inside of the door panel.

7. To make a narrow bed for the dowel rod that holds the door in place, strip the flutes along the vertical ⅜-inch piece on the end of the door panel (point B on the pattern). Wrap the stripped piece around the dowel, giving it a solid color without adding bulk (see figure 4), and glue it in place.

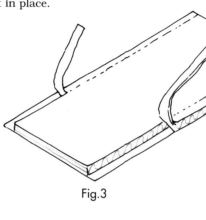

Fig.3

Fig.4

ASSEMBLY

1. Scrape a layer of glue to the center panel of the box body. Cover it with the red back insert.

2. Drizzle a random pattern of glue over the inside of the box body flaps and onto the front and back of the side flaps of the box top and bottom pieces.

3. Assemble the cabinet as you did in Prep step 2, again, using figures 1 and 2 as guides. Don't attach the door at this point, though. You'll

add the door in the Appliqué-tions steps, below.

4. The color can chip or rub off of this sort of cardboard. If necessary, touch up your pieces with the watercolor pens or acrylic paints, then seal the entire cabinet.

APPLIQUÉ-TIONS

FEET AND TOP ADORNMENTS

The cabinet's feet and top adornments, made from double-layer Fold-a-Rolls (Fold-a-Rolls are described on page 25), are simple but will take patience—and hand and wrist muscles. Make two of them red on the outside and yellow on the inside, two yellow on the outside and red on the inside, one blue on the outside and green on the inside, and one green on the outside and blue on the inside.

1. You'll need all 12 of your 1½ x 24-inch colored strips. Run a score line ¼ inch in from the long edge of each strip. Fold over the raw edge and crush it flat (see figure 5). With your thumb and fingers, roll flute by flute, to break the board and make it easier to roll and eventually glue.

2. Separate out the six strips that will be inner strips in the rolls, and finish the edges.

A. On each, open the horizontal fold you made in step 1 and fold over ¼ inch of raw edge on one of the short ends (see figure 6).

B. Clip off one corner of each new vertical fold (see figure 7).

C. Glue down the clipped vertical folds, then fold over and glue down ¼ inch of the long horizontal folds (see figure 8). These short, finished edges will be the starting points for your inner rolls. Roll and glue these edges one rotation to form a core. Mark a line 13 inches in from the unfinished end of each strip.

3. Begin your first double-layer Fold-a-Roll. Cover one inner-strip core with glue. Insert the end of an outer strip into the core (matching the top folded edges, with the uncolored sides up) and wrap the outer strip around the core (see figure 9). Run glue along the widths of both strips, and roll. Wrap tightly, rolling and gluing approximately four times around, until you meet the 13-inch point you marked earlier. Clip off approximately 8½ inches from the unfinished end of the inner strip, leaving a "tail" of approximately 4½ inches. Be sure to save the clipped-off strips; you'll use them later in step 6. Let the glue set before moving on.

4. Fold over the outer strip, sandwiching the shortened inner strip in the fold (see figure 10). Shape this extension into a curl, using the rolls in the project photo as a guide. Repeat the process to make your other five double-layer rolls.

5. You need the 1½ x 7-inch blue strip and 1½ x 8-inch green strip for this step. Wrap and glue the green strip into a loose leaf shape, like the one on top of the cabinet in the project photo. Pinch the ends to keep them pointed. Encase the green leaf shape with the blue strip.

6. Roll and glue the clipped-off strips into small oval feet bases about five layers thick. When you reach the end, strip away about ⅛ inch of cardboard, so you glue down only the strip's top color sheet to finish the oval feet.

7. Use a nail file to roughen up the spots on the cabinet where you'll glue the feet and the top adornment and the spots on the bottom of the feet where you'll glue the oval bases. Glue everything in place.

DOOR

1. If you like, cut a window in your door. Cut the window out of the door's front panel first, then use the cutout piece as a guide for cutting a matching window out of the back panel. Fill the window by using double-stick tape to adhere the vellum sheets to each side of the white card stock and to stick the piece onto the back of the door's front panel.

2. From the colored sheets of E-flute cardboard, cut accent pieces for the door's window and frame. Emboss some of them, if you like, and glue them in place.

3. Scrape an even layer of glue onto the small panel of the door. Press it onto the larger panel, and hold the pieces in place until the bond is secure.

4. Insert the door by working it into the two holes. To create a door stopper, glue together two small circles punched out of single face with your hole punch, then glue the pair just inside the box at the opening of the door. Add another pair at the top.

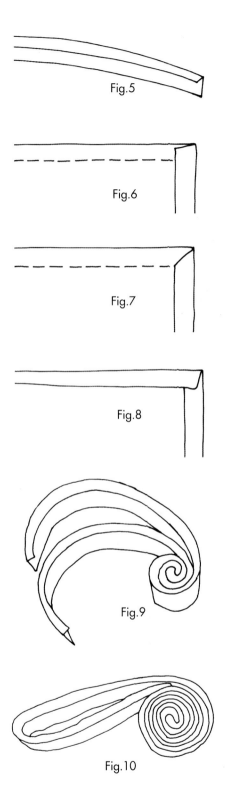

Fig.5

Fig.6

Fig.7

Fig.8

Fig.9

Fig.10

Appliqué-tion Tip:

Keep your Fold-a-Rolls and your oval feet even, or you will have a rockin' curio cabinet!

DIVING BOARD

■ This little cabinet can be made in other sizes to fit your needs. Keep in mind when you work smaller, you may want to use thinner boards, such as E and F flute.

■ Whatever the size of your cabinet, the focal points of the piece are in the rolled adornments and accents on the door. Consider a punched-tin door for a Mexican motif. Your decorative feet and accents could also be rolled from tin or created out of wire balls.

■ Check out the many wire and mesh products now available at both craft and home improvement stores. Why not weave a colorful door from bright colored electrical wire? Add some magnetic strips for movable accents or magnetic poetry. Want to leave a message? Paint your door with chalkboard paint.

■ Add humor to your cabinet's accents. Use silicone (bathroom caulking) in clear or colors to attach game pieces or toys from fast-food meals as feet. Create a tribute to toys by gluing together peaks and spires of characters and their accessories. Still in the game mode? Try folding or rolling playing cards as supports, then store small games and toys in the cabinet.

■ If you need more surface space inside your cabinet, add a cardboard shelf. It should fit snugly in place and look like an upside down "U." Use a double layer of cardboard, so your shelf has adequate strength, and make sure the flutes run in the direction of the shelf depth (front to back).

Flair
Chair

Decorators have flair, fashion designers have flair, the jeans I wore in the 1970s...were ridiculous, but they, too, had flair. Feeling like you need some flair of your own? Then this is the chair for you. The arms, the seat, and the back of this triple-thick cardboard creation get their one-of-a-kind flair from a simple process of partially cutting and stripping the board, leaving it pliable enough to roll.

MATERIALS

CARDBOARD FOR CHAIR

Build your chair out of triple-thick cardboard that has a 58-inch thickness and a 1,100-pound weight designation. This ensures that the board has 1,100 pounds per square inch of pressure capability. In other words, yes, you can really sit in it. To find the sort of sturdy board you need, see the resource list on page 144.

- *Seat front: 27¼ x 23¾ inches*

- *Single seat support: 10⅜ x 14⅛ inches*

- *Slit seat support: 22 x 14⅛ inches*

- *Seat back and arms: 36¾ x 49¼ inches*

OTHER MATERIALS

Flair Chair patterns, pages 140 & 142

Approximately 1 yard of fabric in a pattern of your choice

Fabric glue or premixed fabric wallpaper paste

Craft glue

TOOLS

Cutting mat

Metal ruler or T-square

Craft knife and extra blades, lots of blades or jigsaw

Tweezers (optional)

SUGGESTED REREADING

Slit Scores, page 21

PREP

1. Transfer the patterns to the cardboard, and cut out all your pieces. Cut the slit score on the seat support.

2. The method of partial cutting and stripping that allows this chair's thick cardboard to roll is simple. First, following the pattern markings, draw lines on your seat back and arms piece and your seat front piece to mark out slats and grooves. The slats should be 1½ inches wide and the grooves ¼ inch wide. With your metal ruler and very sharp blades in your craft knife, carefully cut your lines on all the pieces, then strip away two layers of the board in the grooves (see photos 1 and 2). You may need your craft knife to pick out the start of the strip. Tweezers are also handy for pulling out the strips. And the good news is, the cutting and stripping are hidden in the final chair, so neither neatness nor perfection is critical.

3. After stripping all the grooves, roll the slatted pieces, rolling the grooves onto themselves.

4. Flip over the seat back and arms piece. You're now working on the front of the piece. Cut the two ½-inch wide recessed notches marked A on the pattern. Instead of cutting these notches through just two layers, cut through to the last sheet of the board's paper (but not through the paper). Be sure to cut the angled slit at the top of each notch, which eases the board and helps prevent tearing when you bring the seat arms forward in the final assembly.

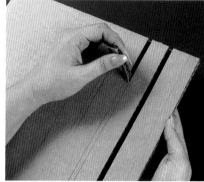

PHOTO 1

PHOTO 2

CUTTING AND STRIPPING GROOVES IN A PIECE OF THICK CARDBOARD ALLOW IT TO ROLL.

5. Still working on the front of the piece, cut out the recessed-notch T slot indicated on the pattern. If you don't want the T slot to show in the back of the chair, you can simply strip out this T shape through two layers of cardboard. Or, you can use appliqués to cover the back of this spot later.

TEST ASSEMBLY

This is only a test. This is not the real assembly. The real assembly will take place after the test assembly. By test-assembling first, you avoid gluing and then removing glue from joints that don't quite fit. Use figure 1 as an assembly guide.

1. Fold the arm ends of the seat back panel forward. The width of each panel nests in the recessed A

notches, to make a flush back panel and covered fold joint. If you don't nest the panels in the grooves, your chair's seat area will be too wide.

2. Slide the angled back end of the slit seat support into the base of the recessed T slot in the center of the seat back. Pull panel B of the seat support back from the slit score until it's flush with the side of the support. Insert the single seat support into the open edge of the slit score.

3. Slide the seat in place, inserting the chair arms into the slots of the seat, and the tab at the back of the seat into the top of the recessed T slot in the seat back.

4. Once you're satisfied with how all your pieces fit together, skip down to Appliqué-tions and add your chair's embellishments. Finally, unassemble the chair, add glue to all the slots, and reassemble it permanently.

APPLIQUÉ-TIONS

1. Cut fabric pieces to decorate your chair's seat, back, and arms. For the chair pictured here, I chose a fabric featuring vertical stripes, to echo the shape of the chair's slats. However, you may choose to use blocks of solid-colored fabric, patches of fabric polka dots, or panels of a bold ethnic-print fabric. You can use the project photo as a guide and cut your fabric pieces in roughly the same size as mine, or you can cut pieces that work better for the design you have in mind.

2. Glue your fabric embellishments in place. The material I used was rather thick, so the glue didn't show through. If you're working with a more delicate or sheer material, test your glue or try fabric wallpaper paste. One warning: Some wallpaper paste will leave a stain on your material if you're not careful.

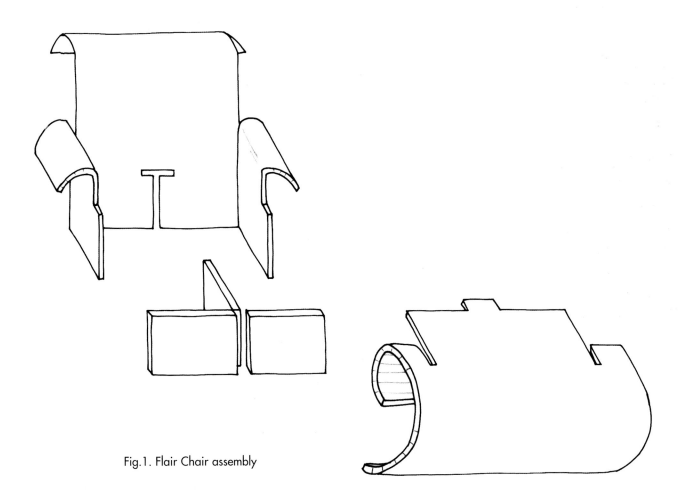

Fig.1. Flair Chair assembly

Metric Equivalents

½"	1.3 cm
⅝"	1.6 cm
10⅜"	26.4 cm
14"	35.6 cm
14⅛"	35.9 cm
22"	56 cm
23¾"	60.3 cm
27¼"	69.2 cm
36¾"	93.3 cm
49¼"	125 cm
1 yard	0.9 m
1,100 lbs	500 kg

DIVING BOARD

■ If you'd like your chair's arms to curl rather than flair, try using some of the wild and colorful shoelaces available today to tie them down.

■ You can give your chair real life by gluing an old pair of favorite shorts on the seat and a shirt on the back, then stuffing them to make a padded chair. Or, sticking with the clothing theme, try weaving together a variety of wide and skinny thrift-store ties for a seat cushion.

■ Want to avoid all the cutting and stripping it takes to create this chair's flaired arms, back, and seat front? Instead, strip just one or two slits in each piece to angle it rather than give it full-blown flair.

■ For a more substantial-looking chair, pad the arms with pieces of polyester batting, then cover the batting with fabric.

Ms. Divine
Divan

This couch, like its name, demands attention. It's a seat of power, a courting chair, and a classic fainting couch. Dedicated to an incredible crafter, whom I lovingly call Ms. Divine, it characterizes her whimsical approach, her stolid character, and her sense of tradition—not to mention her strength. Though it looks to be the

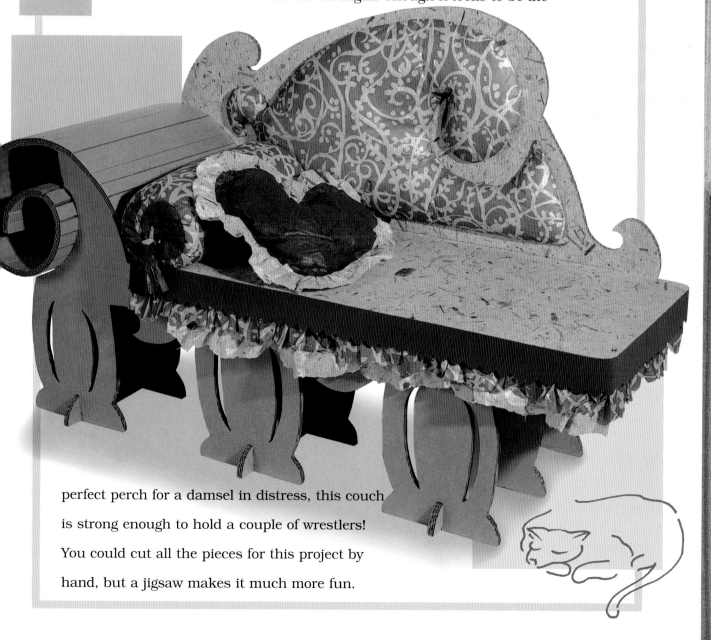

perfect perch for a damsel in distress, this couch is strong enough to hold a couple of wrestlers! You could cut all the pieces for this project by hand, but a jigsaw makes it much more fun.

MATERIALS

CARDBOARD FOR COUCH

Build your couch out of triple-thick cardboard made of two layers of A flute and one layer of C flute with a 1,100-pound weight designation. This ensures that the board as has 1,100 pounds per square inch of pressure capability. In other words, yes, you, can really sit on it. To find the sort of sturdy board you need, see the resource list on page 144.

- *Couch back: 52¼ x 36¼ inches*

- *Middle seat panel: 52¼ x 24½ inches*

- *Front seat panel: 52¼ x 24½ inches*

- *Seat supports: 2 measuring 19¼ x 16 inches and 1 measuring 19¼ x 14 inches*

- *Arc roll panel: 46 x 19 inches*

- *Seat: 41½ x 19 inches*

CARDBOARD AND PAPER FOR APPLIQUÉ-TIONS

- *1 sheet of B-flute cardboard, 17 x 35 inches*

- *2 sheets of patterned handmade paper*

- *4 sheets of handmade banana paper in green*

- *2 sheets of handmade banana paper in burgundy*

- *4 sheets of single-face cardboard in colors that match or contrast with your other papers*

OTHER MATERIALS

Ms. Divine Divan patterns, page 143

Craft glue or glue gun and glue sticks

Rubber cement

Rubber cement remover

1 bag of polyester fiberfill

TOOLS

Hand-held jigsaw with a fine blade

Craft knife

Cutting mat

Metal ruler or T-square

Scissors

Decorative-edge scissors

SUGGESTED REREADING

Transfers to Success, page 16

Scoring, page 19

Metric Equivalents

½"	1.3 cm
1⅛"	2.8 cm
2½"	6.4 cm
3"	7.6 cm
5"	12.7 cm
14"	35.6 cm
16"	40.6 cm
17"	43.2 cm
19"	48.3 cm
19¼"	48.9 cm
24½"	62.2 cm
35"	88.9 cm
36¼"	92 cm
41½"	105.4 cm
46"	116.8 cm
52¼"	132.7 cm
1,100 lbs	500 kg

PREP

1. Transfer all the couch patterns to the triple-wall cardboard, and cut the pieces out with the jigsaw. Note that you need to cut one of the seat supports 2 inches shorter than the others; this shorter cut mark is designated by a dotted line on the seat support pattern.

2. On the arc roll panel, mark slit scores 1⅛ inches apart and parallel with the fluting. Cut the slit scores through all layers but the bottom sheet of paper. Line up your metal ruler with your first score line and run a very sharp blade lightly over the line, cutting through the top layer of paper. Run it through a second and a third time. When you think you are close to the bottom sheet of paper, lift the board and try to break the slit open. If it doesn't open easily, run your blade through the partial slit until the board snaps but the outer wrap of the paper remains intact, acting like a hinge. Continue this process to create all the slit scores.

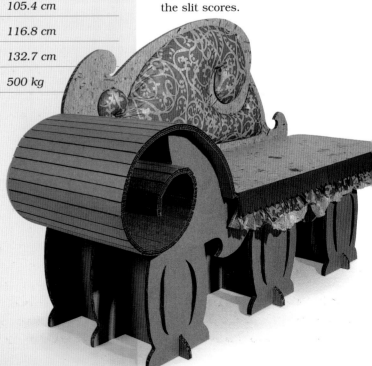

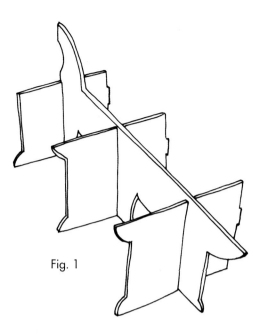

Fig. 1

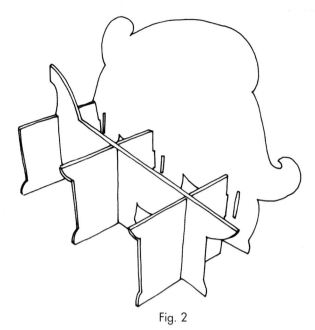

Fig. 2

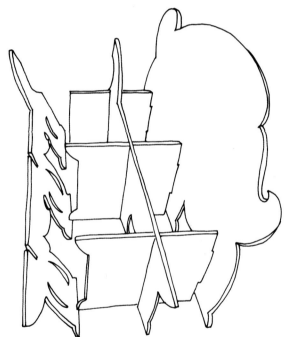

Fig. 3

ASSEMBLY

1. Slide the seat supports onto the middle seat panel, aligning the slots and pushing the panel down until it's flush with the bottom of the supports (see figure 1). The shorter support goes at the arced end of the seat panel.

2. Fit the notches on the seat supports into the slots of the couch back (see figure 2).

3. Attach the front seat panel by sliding its slots over the feet of the seat supports (see figure 3).

4. Place the couch seat onto the frame you've created. The tab at one end of the seat sits against the arced end of the middle seat panel.

5. Place the arc roll over the arc of the frame, fitting its notch over the tab on the seat. The arc roll will naturally roll into shape.

6. Before gluing anything, determine whether you need to tweak any of your pieces to create a bet-

ter-fitting assembly. If you do, make the adjustments now. Then, skip ahead to Appliqué-tions and add your embellishments before gluing your couch together. Finally, glue all the couch's joints and notches using craft glue or a glue gun. Glue the arc roll onto the raw edges of the arced portions of the middle and

front seat panels (markings A and B on the patterns). Let all the glue dry thoroughly before you start fainting!

APPLIQUÉ-TIONS

For the couch shown here, I created a series of embellishments that amplify the lines of the couch design. Could you go more extreme?

Of course! Also, I used only paper products, but you could pad your whole piece and cover it with fabric.

COUCH BACK

Adding a small, stuffed piece on the couch back is a more manageable undertaking than covering the whole piece.

1. Cut the couch back detail out of B-flute cardboard.

2. Cover the couch back detail with a layer of stuffing, and glue the stuffing in place.

3. Place one sheet of patterned handmade paper over the back detail, covering all the edges and nooks. Ease your rounded edges with scissors. Start on the flat edge of the detail panel and glue the paper down gradually around the perimeter of the piece. You will need to add small strips of paper in the big swirl to close gaps created by easing the slits. These small strips come from leftover scrap from the sheet of handmade paper.

4. Cover the couch back with the green banana paper by stippling on craft glue and laying the paper down. If you want a seamless look, tear the edge of the paper along the side being seamed, and slightly overlap the edges.

5. When the glue dries, trim off the excess paper. Center and glue down the couch back detail, and lay it flat to dry.

COUCH SEAT

Simply glue down two sheets of banana paper on the seat. Seam the paper, again, by tearing the edge of one piece and slightly overlapping the two.

FRINGE

1. Cut strips of burgundy single face, 2½ inches wide. Make one end of each strip straight; cut the other with large decorative-edge scissors. You need enough strips to create one long strip that will fit along the front and end of the seat. Seam the strips together, matching the scissor-cut pattern.

2. Cut strips of the patterned handmade paper, 3 inches wide, and glue them down on the back of the burgundy strips about ½ inch down from the straight edge of the burgundy strip. As you glue, pinch the handmade paper to ruffle the trim. You can create a seamless skirt by gluing back the end of each paper strip and starting the new strip at this same point. Your finished paper strips should resemble the folds of a skirt.

3. Cut strips of green banana paper, 5 inches wide, and glue them down so they extend as a second ruffle below the handmade paper.

4. Glue the skirt around the perimeter of the seat.

DIVING BOARD

SOLO DIVING

In this last diving board of the book, let me encourage you to jump in with both feet and follow your own instincts when it comes to embellishing your couch. Focus on its fanciful shape, and let your imagination go. Following are a few suggestions to get you started if you'd like to come up with your own Appliqué-tions.

■ Cover your entire couch with cloth, then surprise people by telling them what's underneath.

■ For a contemporary twist, use spray paint to cover the surface of your couch with graffiti-style images and words.

■ Use elegant handmade papers to decoupage your couch.

■ Leave off the back for a completely different look.

Patterns

Red arrows on patterns indicate fluting direction.

Inverse Temple Bowl Pattern

Actual Size

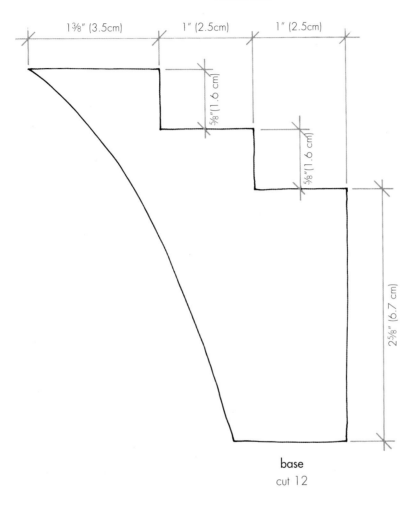

1⅜" (3.5cm)   1" (2.5cm)   1" (2.5cm)

⅝" (1.6 cm)

⅝" (1.6 cm)

2⅝" (6.7 cm)

base

cut 12

Punch & Jewelry Pattern

Actual Size

bead

E-Zeemoney Patterns

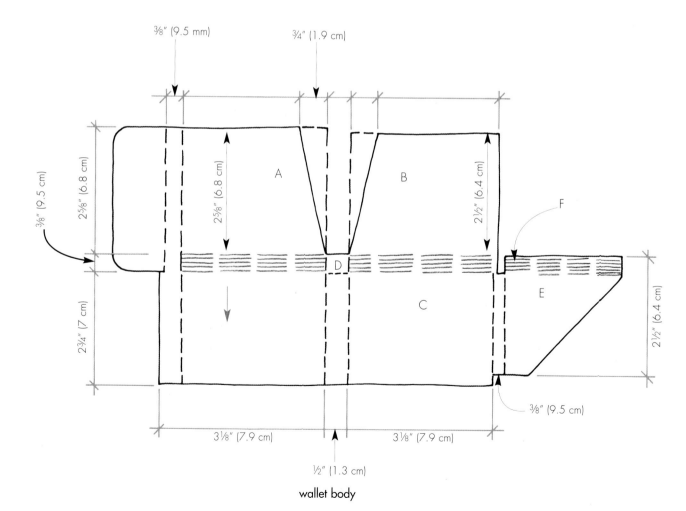

7/8" (2.2 cm)   5/8" (1.6 cm)   1/4" (6 mm)

2¾" (6.7 cm)

3½" (8.9 cm)

H

G   G

coin case

H

3/8" (9.5 mm)   ¾" (1.9 cm)

3/8" (9.5 cm)

2⅝" (6.8 cm)

2⅝" (6.8 cm)

2½" (6.4 cm)

A   B

F

2¾" (7 cm)

D

C   E

2½" (6.4 cm)

3/8" (9.5 cm)

3⅛" (7.9 cm)   3⅛" (7.9 cm)

½" (1.3 cm)

wallet body

Whirlwined Patterns

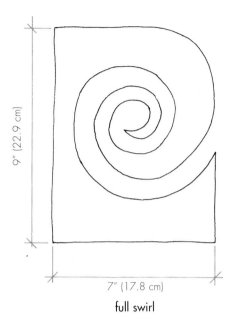

9" (22.9 cm)

7" (17.8 cm)

loose swirl

9" (22.9 cm)

7" (17.8 cm)

full swirl

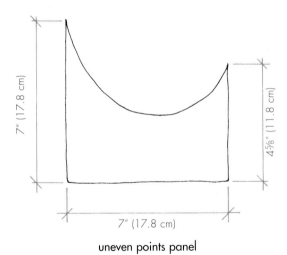

7" (17.8 cm)

4⅝" (11.8 cm)

7" (17.8 cm)

uneven points panel

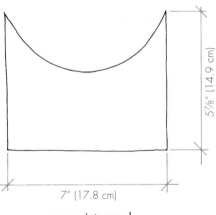

5⅞" (14.9 cm)

7" (17.8 cm)

even points panel

Make a Stand Patterns

corner detail
enlarge 200%

Ha, Ha, Ha Hall Light Patterns

bell
enlarge 200%

cut on fold

paper ears

enlarge so straight side is approximately
11 ½" (29.2 cm.)

3" (7.6 cm)

9" (22.9 cm)

1" (2.5 cm)
corner roll

Hangin' Around Patterns

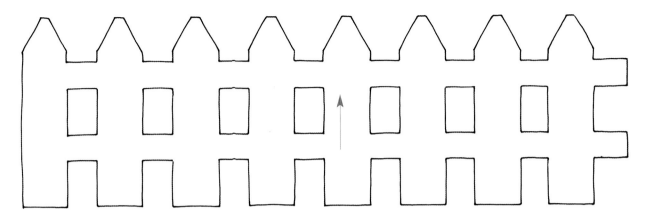

fence
enlarge 200%

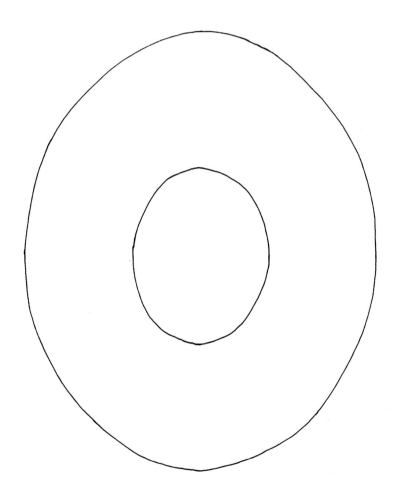

Ovalette
actual size

Rosie Bedosie Patterns

Enlarge 200%

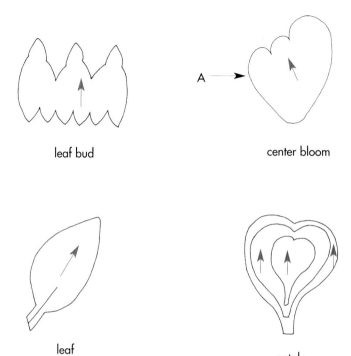

leaf bud

center bloom

leaf

cut with decorative-edge scissors

petals

Baby Bedosie Patterns

Enlarge 200%

center bud

leaf bud

Ivy League Patterns

Actual Size

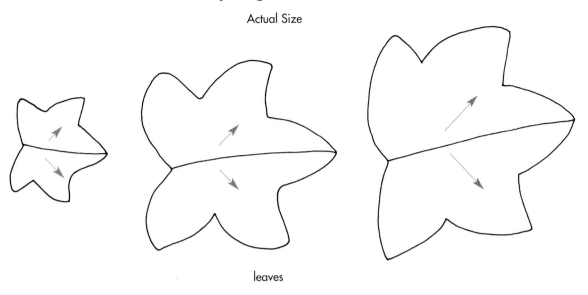

leaves

Fuzzy Hot Dog Patterns

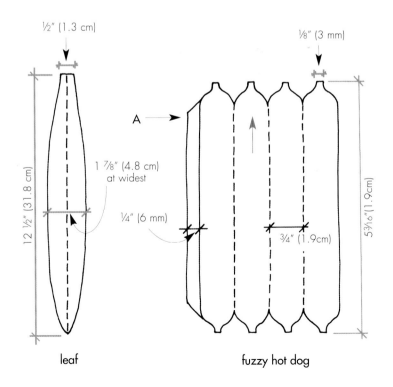

leaf   fuzzy hot dog

Mum's the Word Patterns

Actual Size

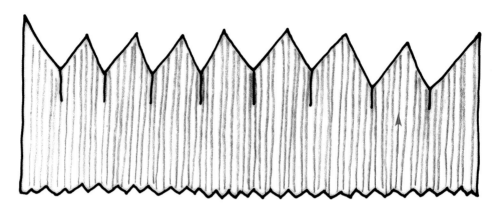

base stem

124

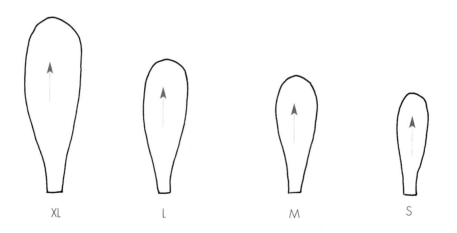

XL   L   M   S

petals

Call of the Wild Patterns

Enlarge 200%

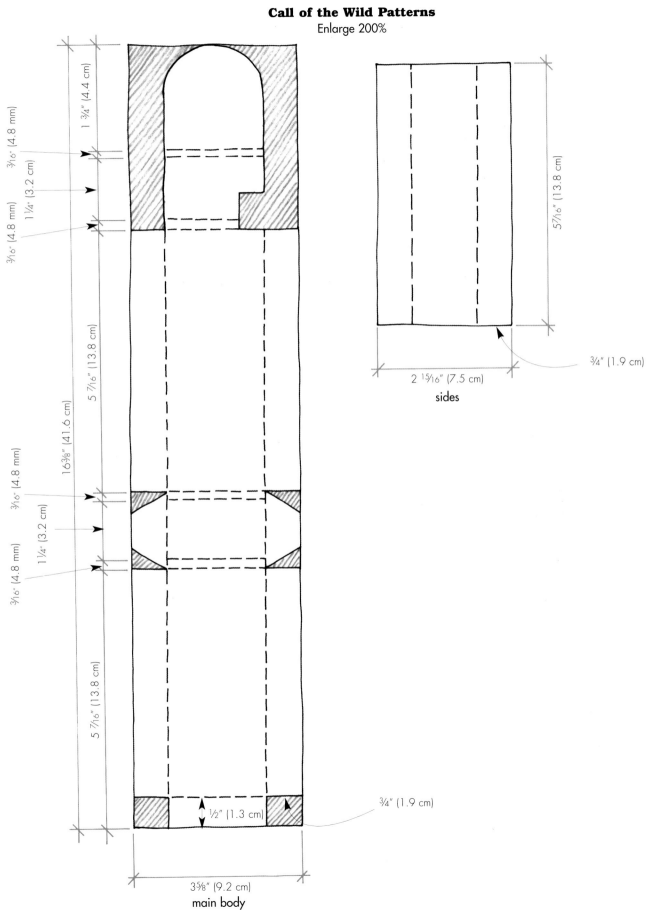

1 ¾" (4.4 cm)

³⁄₁₆" (4.8 mm)

1 ¼" (3.2 cm)

³⁄₁₆" (4.8 mm)

5 ⁷⁄₁₆" (13.8 cm)

16 ³⁄₈" (41.6 cm)

³⁄₁₆" (4.8 mm)

1 ¼" (3.2 cm)

³⁄₁₆" (4.8 mm)

5 ⁷⁄₁₆" (13.8 cm)

½" (1.3 cm)

¾" (1.9 cm)

3 ⁵⁄₈" (9.2 cm)

main body

5 ⁷⁄₁₆" (13.8 cm)

¾" (1.9 cm)

2 ¹⁵⁄₁₆" (7.5 cm)

sides

125

Call of the Wild Patterns

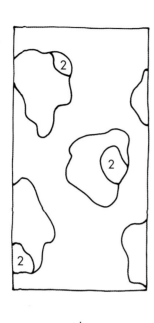

sides

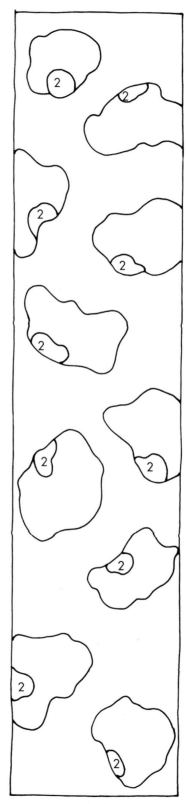

main body

animal-print patterns

Mask of Gazelle-Da Patterns

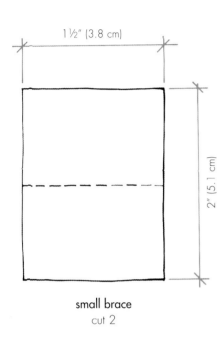

1½" (3.8 cm)

2" (5.1 cm)

small brace
cut 2

braces

1½" (3.8 cm)

1¹⁄₁₆" (1.7 cm)

3¼" (8.3 cm)

4⅝" (11.7 cm)

1¹⁄₁₆" (1.7 cm)

large brace
cut 1

4⅜"(11.1cm)   5"(12.7cm)   ⅛"(3mm)

B   B

2"(5.1cm)

A

2¼"(5.7cm)

3⅞"(9.8cm)

19¼"(48.9cm)

128

4"(10.2cm)

13¾"(34.9cm)

mask

Mask of Gazelle-Da Appliqué Patterns
All Actual Size Unless Measurement Noted

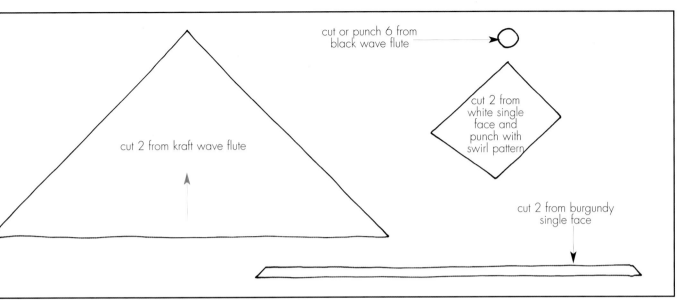

cut or punch 6 from black wave flute

cut 2 from white single face and punch with swirl pattern

cut 2 from kraft wave flute

cut 2 from burgundy single face

side of nose detail

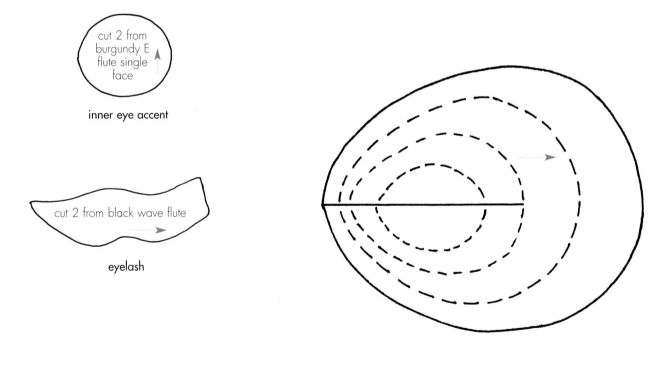

cut 2 from burgundy E flute single face

inner eye accent

cut 2 from black wave flute

eyelash

eye
cut 2 from kraft E flute single face

Mask of Gazelle-Da Appliqué Patterns

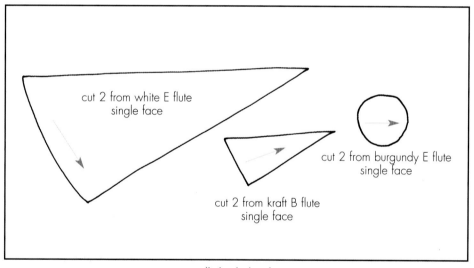

cut 2 from black wave flute

cut 2 from kraft E flute single face

cut 2 from white E flute single face

cut 2 from ochre B flute single face

cut or punch 2 from ochre B flute single face

cut 6 from burgundy E flute single face

ear detail

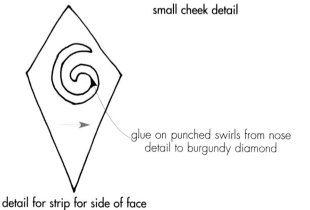

cut 2 from white E flute single face

cut 2 from kraft B flute single face

cut 2 from burgundy E flute single face

small cheek detail

forehead detail

cut 2 from burgundy E flute single face and punch hole in center, glue fluting side down

glue on punched swirls from nose detail to burgundy diamond

side of face details

cut 6 from burgundy E flute single face

detail for strip for side of face

cut 2 from burgundy single face

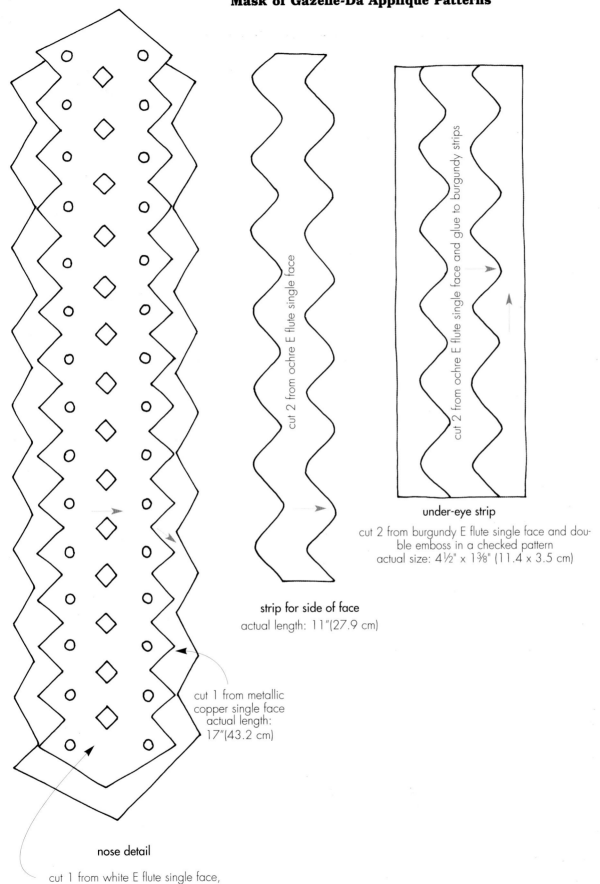

cut 2 from ochre E flute single face

cut 2 from ochre E flute single face and glue to burgundy strips

under-eye strip

cut 2 from burgundy E flute single face and double emboss in a checked pattern
actual size: 4½" x 1⅜" (11.4 x 3.5 cm)

cut 1 from metallic copper single face
actual length: 17"(43.2 cm)

strip for side of face
actual length: 11"(27.9 cm)

nose detail

cut 1 from white E flute single face,
punch holes, double emboss, and glue to copper strip
actual length: 16" (40.6 cm)

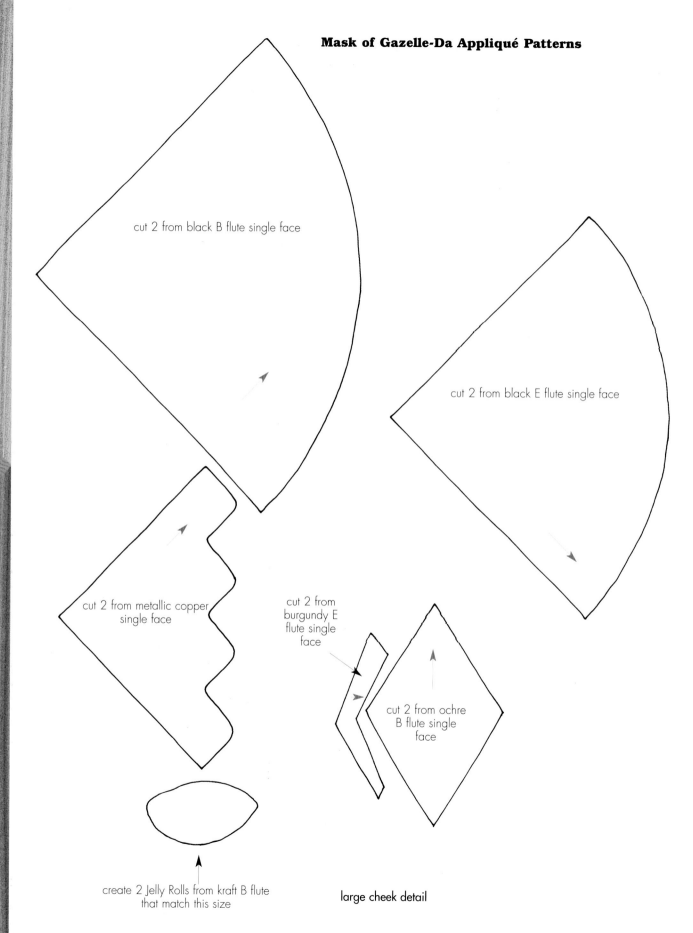

cut 2 from black B flute single face

cut 2 from black E flute single face

cut 2 from metallic copper
single face

cut 2 from
burgundy E
flute single
face

cut 2 from ochre
B flute single
face

create 2 Jelly Rolls from kraft B flute
that match this size

large cheek detail

United We Stand Divider Patterns

Enlarge to Desired Size

Forest Trunk Patterns

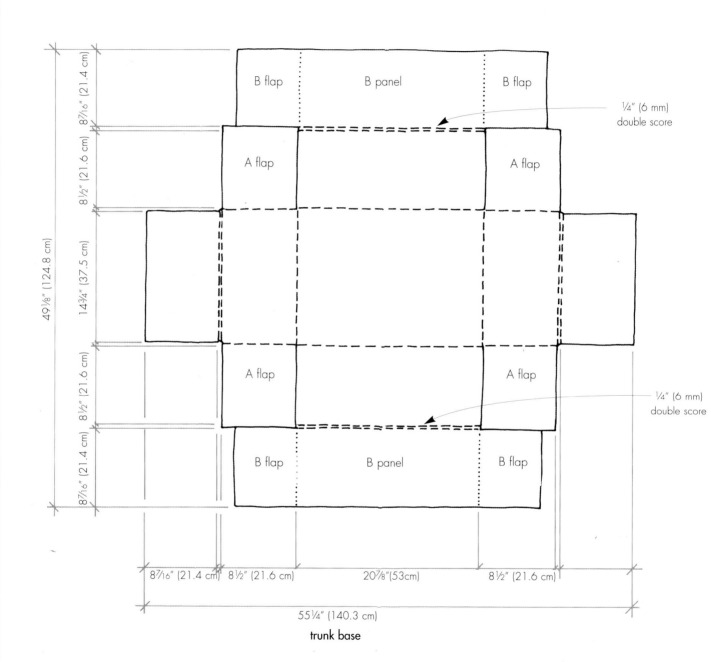

B flap   B panel   B flap

¼" (6 mm)
double score

A flap   A flap

8⅞₁₆" (21.4 cm)

8½" (21.6 cm)

49⅛" (124.8 cm)   14¾" (37.5 cm)

A flap   A flap

¼" (6 mm)
double score

8½" (21.6 cm)

8⅞₁₆" (21.4 cm)

B flap   B panel   B flap

8⅞₁₆" (21.4 cm)   8½" (21.6 cm)   20⅞"(53cm)   8½" (21.6 cm)

55¼" (140.3 cm)

trunk base

Forest Trunk Patterns

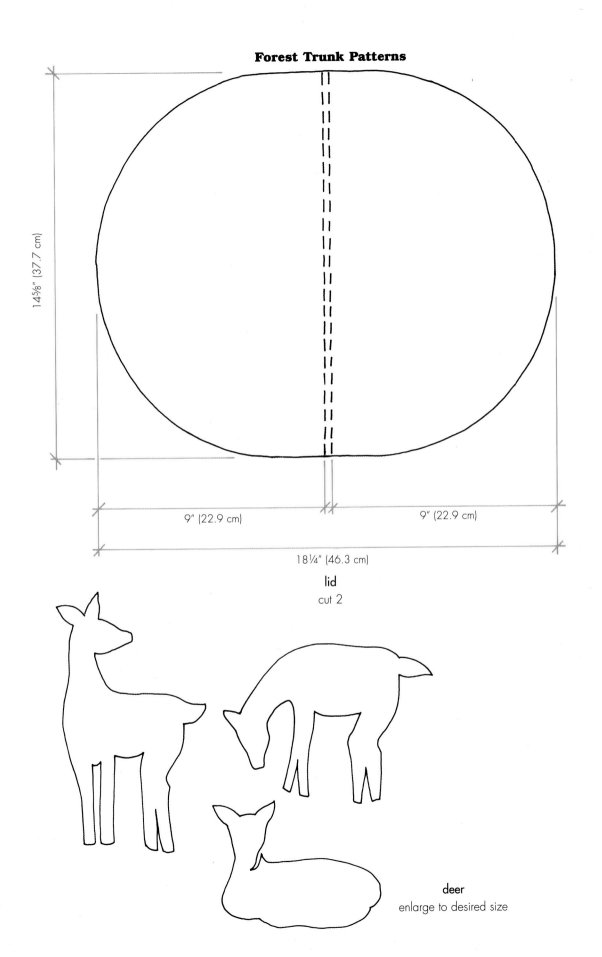

14⅝" (37.7 cm)

9" (22.9 cm)

9" (22.9 cm)

18¼" (46.3 cm)

lid
cut 2

deer
enlarge to desired size

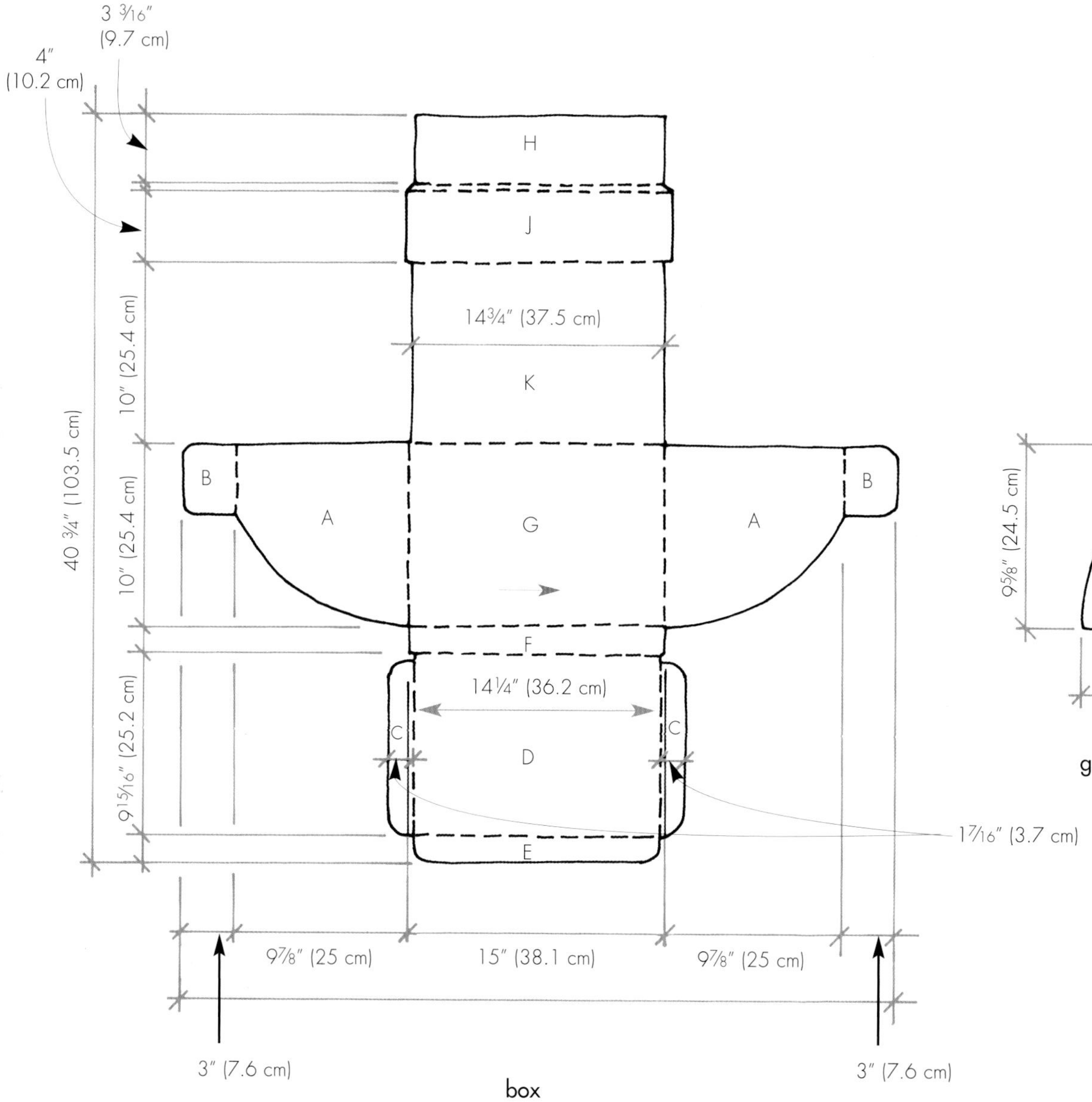

3 ³⁄₁₆″
(9.7 cm)

4″
(10.2 cm)

40 ¾″ (103.5 cm)

10″ (25.4 cm)

10″ (25.4 cm)

9¹⁵⁄₁₆″ (25.2 cm)

H

J

14¾″ (37.5 cm)

K

B

A

G

A

B

F

14¼″ (36.2 cm)

C

D

C

E

1⁷⁄₁₆″ (3.7 cm)

9⅞″ (25 cm)

15″ (38.1 cm)

9⅞″ (25 cm)

3″ (7.6 cm)

3″ (7.6 cm)

box

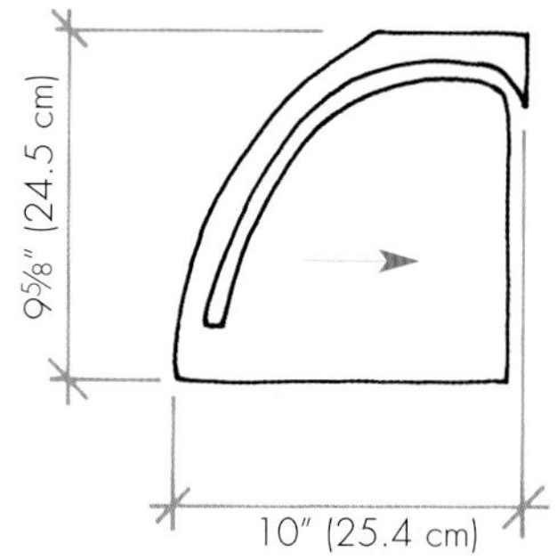

9⅝″ (24.5 cm)

10″ (25.4 cm)

groove side panels
cut 4

136

French Groove Rolltop Desk Appliqué Patterns

Actual Size Unless Measurement Noted

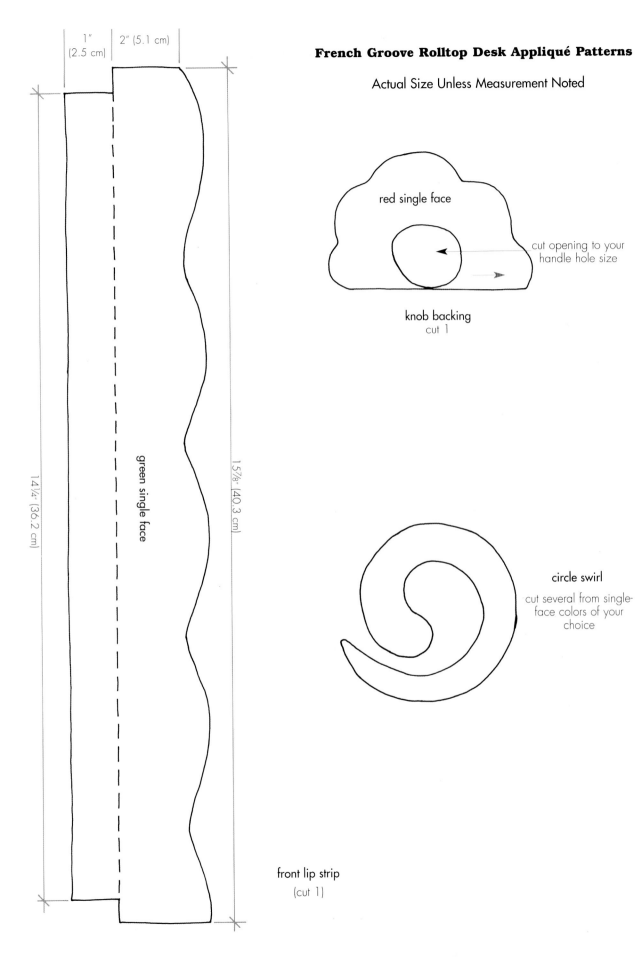

1" (2.5 cm)

2" (5.1 cm)

14¼" (36.2 cm)

15⅞" (40.3 cm)

green single face

front lip strip

(cut 1)

red single face

cut opening to your handle hole size

knob backing
cut 1

circle swirl

cut several from single-face colors of your choice

French Groove Rolltop Desk Appliqué Patterns

Actual Size Unless Measurement Noted

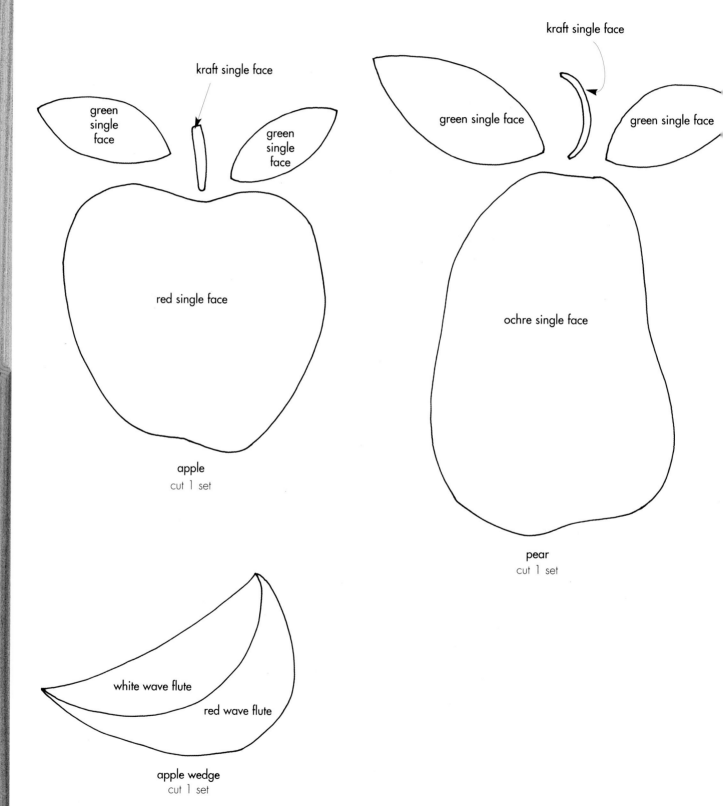

kraft single face

green single face

green single face

red single face

apple
cut 1 set

kraft single face

green single face

green single face

ochre single face

pear
cut 1 set

white wave flute

red wave flute

apple wedge
cut 1 set

French Groove Rolltop Desk Appliqué Patterns
Actual Size Unless Measurement Noted

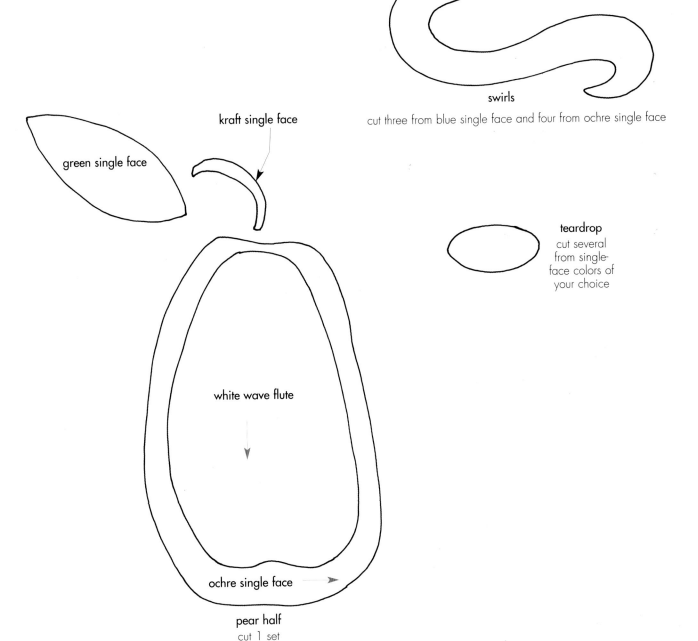

swirls

cut three from blue single face and four from ochre single face

green single face

kraft single face

teardrop

cut several from single-face colors of your choice

white wave flute

ochre single face

pear half

cut 1 set

Curlicue Curio Cabinet Patterns

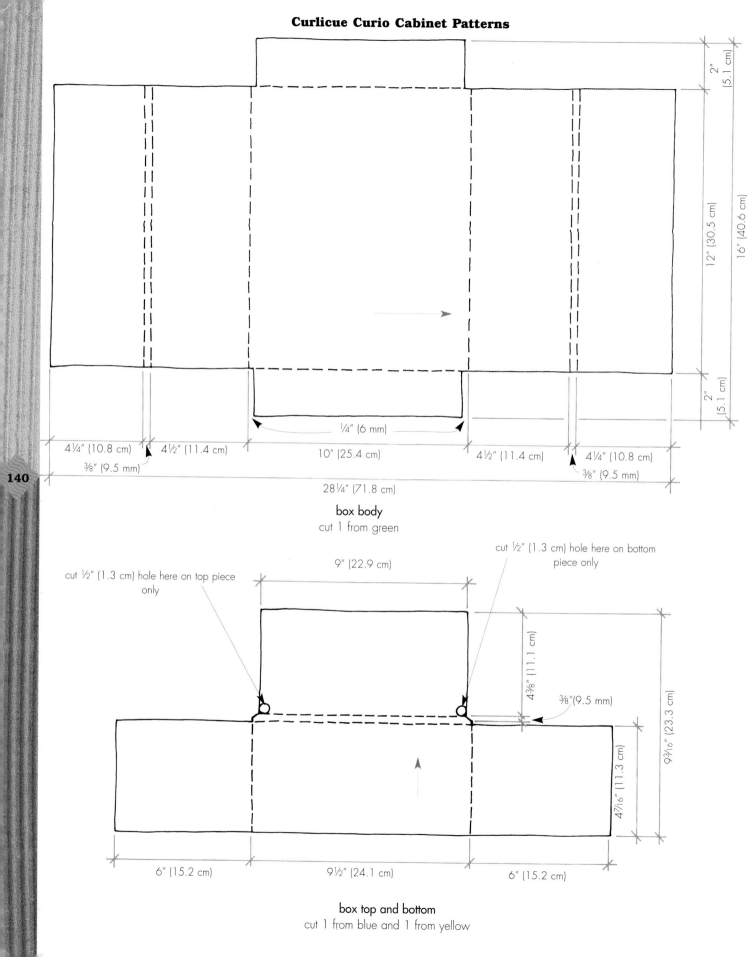

2" (5.1 cm)

16" (40.6 cm)

12" (30.5 cm)

2" (5.1 cm)

¼" (6 mm)

4¼" (10.8 cm)   4½" (11.4 cm)   10" (25.4 cm)   4½" (11.4 cm)   4¼" (10.8 cm)

⅜" (9.5 mm)   ⅜" (9.5 mm)

28¼" (71.8 cm)

box body
cut 1 from green

cut ½" (1.3 cm) hole here on bottom piece only

9" (22.9 cm)

cut ½" (1.3 cm) hole here on top piece only

4⅜" (11.1 cm)

⅜" (9.5 mm)

9³⁄₁₆" (23.3 cm)

4⁷⁄₁₆" (11.3 cm)

6" (15.2 cm)   9½" (24.1 cm)   6" (15.2 cm)

box top and bottom
cut 1 from blue and 1 from yellow

Curlicue Curio Cabinet Patterns

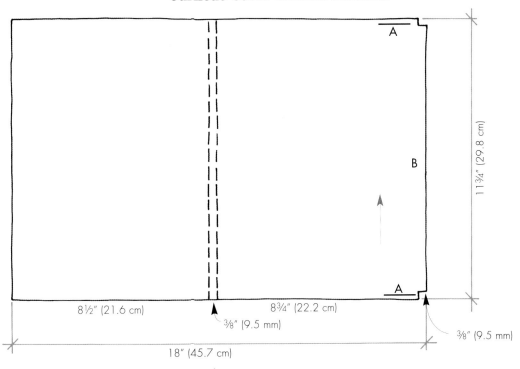

8½" (21.6 cm)   8¾" (22.2 cm)

⅜" (9.5 mm)

⅜" (9.5 mm)

11¾" (29.8 cm)

18" (45.7 cm)

door

cut 1 from red

Flair Chair Patterns

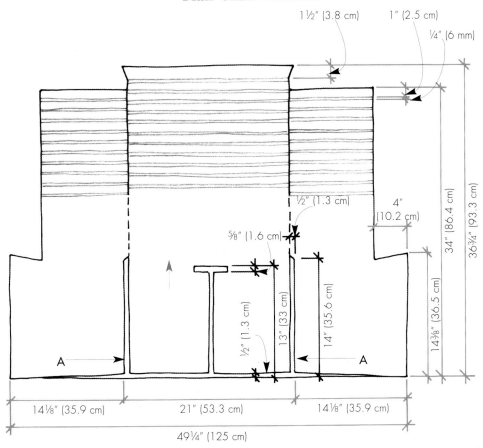

1½" (3.8 cm)   1" (2.5 cm)

¼" (6 mm)

½" (1.3 cm)

⅝" (1.6 cm)

4" (10.2 cm)

½" (1.3 cm)

13" (33 cm)

14" (35.6 cm)

34" (86.4 cm)

36¾" (93.3 cm)

14⅜" (36.5 cm)

14⅛" (35.9 cm)   21" (53.3 cm)   14⅛" (35.9 cm)

49¼" (125 cm)

seat back and arms

Flair Chair Patterns

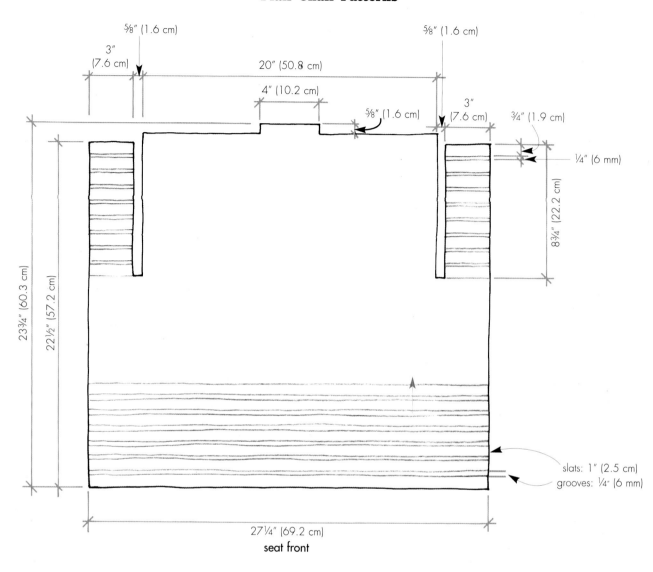

⅝" (1.6 cm) ⅝" (1.6 cm)

3"
(7.6 cm)

20" (50.8 cm)

4" (10.2 cm)

⅝" (1.6 cm)

3"
(7.6 cm)

¾" (1.9 cm)

¼" (6 mm)

8¾" (22.2 cm)

23¾" (60.3 cm)

22½" (57.2 cm)

slats: 1" (2.5 cm)
grooves: ¼" (6 mm)

27¼" (69.2 cm)

seat front

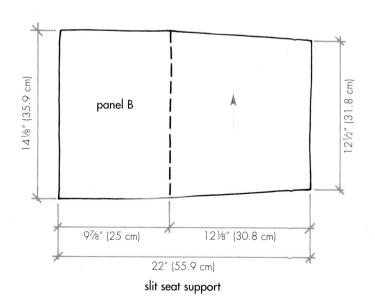

14⅛" (35.9 cm)

panel B

12½" (31.8 cm)

9⅞" (25 cm)

12⅛" (30.8 cm)

22" (55.9 cm)

slit seat support

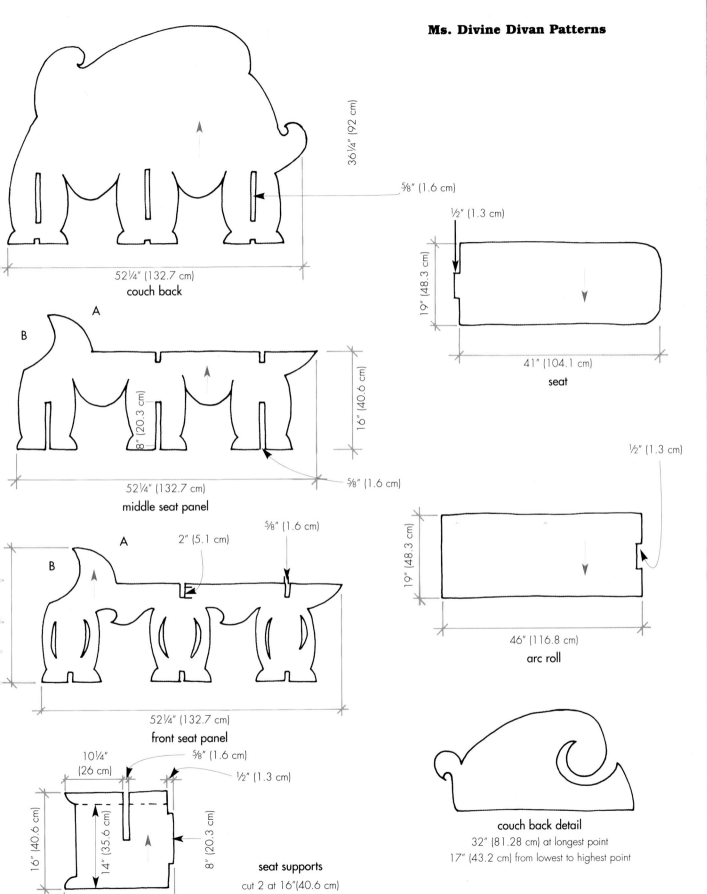

36¼" (92 cm)

5⁄8" (1.6 cm)

52¼" (132.7 cm)

couch back

½" (1.3 cm)

19" (48.3 cm)

41" (104.1 cm)

seat

A

B

8" (20.3 cm)

16" (40.6 cm)

52¼" (132.7 cm)

5⁄8" (1.6 cm)

middle seat panel

A

2" (5.1 cm)

5⁄8" (1.6 cm)

B

52¼" (132.7 cm)

front seat panel

½" (1.3 cm)

19" (48.3 cm)

46" (116.8 cm)

arc roll

10¼" (26 cm)

5⁄8" (1.6 cm)

½" (1.3 cm)

16" (40.6 cm)

14" (35.6 cm)

8" (20.3 cm)

19¼" (48.8 cm)

seat supports
cut 2 at 16"(40.6 cm)
cut 1 at 14"(35.6 cm)

couch back detail
32" (81.28 cm) at longest point
17" (43.2 cm) from lowest to highest point

Acknowledgments

It is odd to me that a single name appears on a book's cover when there are so many people involved in putting that book together. I met only a few of the people involved in this book, and I would like to thank them now. Thanks, too, to the many people at Lark Books I did not have the pleasure of meeting in person. (Does this sound like the beginning of a horrid award speech, or what?)

I'll start with Lark Books President Rob Pulleyn; Publishing Director Carol Taylor; and Editor and Project Coordinator Terry Taylor. The three happened upon our Mixed Nuts booth at a craft show several years ago and saw a seed of a book in my work, then gave me the opportunity to create that book. Thanks, too, to Dana Irwin, the book's art director, Thom Gaines and Hannes Charen, her assistants, and Evan Bracken and Sandra Stambaugh, the photographers, who handled my work as if it were cast gold. My admiration and love go to my phenomenal editor, Paige Gilchrist, a gift from beyond, whose talent and patience let her wade through pages of randomly strung words and transform my babble into understandable thought bubbles. Thank you just doesn't seem enough. Paige: Do you have a word I could use?

I need to personally thank two of my dear friends who took the time to devote their work toward my dreams, and who made everything easier. Tami Cox, your smile and typing speed made my drafting and rewriting effortless, and your incredible ability to translate my scribbles is remarkable. (I'm working on the shape of my r's.) You are a diamond to my whole family. Steve Castro, I appreciate your masterful translation of my drawings into computer renderings so others can actually use them to make something. You're brilliant, and I thank you for never questioning my sanity.

Mom and Dad, thank you for all the crayons and other craft supplies you gave me when I was young, and I'm sorry for the times I made *you* question my sanity!

I have a special note to my friend, Wes. I will admit here and only here that, yes, I did lose my first game to you on my cardboard chessboard, but dare I speak of what happened in the rematches?

I have saved the best for last—my best friend, confidante, business partner, and best of all, my sister, Diane. I love you and thank you for letting me create this book (and for not deducting the time I spent on it from my paycheck!).

Also, special thanks to **DMS** industries, www.dmsind.com, for donating decorative-flute cardboards and to **Emagination,** www.emaginationcrafts.com, for the hole punches used in projects throughout the book.

Resources

MIXED NUTS, 221 Rayon Drive, Old Hickory, TN 37138 ▪ Fax: 615-847-5475, E-mail: mixednuts@mindspring.com ▪Website: crazycardboard.com

Mixed Nuts can provide you with Boardering the Norm Frames, Ring-a-Ding Dings, and Ovalettes (all optional purchases for various projects in the Leg Up chapter, beginning on page 47). They can also supply you with triple-thick cardboard sheets.